It's another great book from CGP...

Maths exams can seem daunting — especially if you're not sure what to expect.
But they're less stressful if you've done plenty of realistic practice in advance.

Happily, this book (which includes a **free** Online Edition)
is packed with exam-style questions to fully prepare you for the real thing.
We've even thrown in practice exams with online video solutions.

How to get your free online extras

Want to read this book on your computer or tablet?
Just go to **cgpbooks.co.uk/extras** and enter this code...

0633 9795 0272 1825

By the way, this code only works for one person. If somebody else has used
this book before you, they might have already claimed the online extras.

CGP — still the best! ☺

Our sole aim here at CGP is to produce the highest quality books —
carefully written, immaculately presented and dangerously close to being funny.

Then we work our socks off to get them out to you
— at the cheapest possible prices.

Contents

☑ Use the tick boxes to check off the topics you've completed.

Section Five — Angles and Geometry

Section Six — Measures

Section Seven — Statistics and Probability

Practice Papers

How to get answers for the Practice Papers
Your free Online Edition of this book includes a link to step-by-step video solutions
for Practice Papers 1 & 2, plus worked solutions you can print out.
(Just flick back to the previous page to find out how to get hold of your Online Edition.)

Published by CGP

Editors:
Katherine Craig, Kirstie McHale, Sarah Oxley, Sam Pilgrim,
David Ryan, Megan Tyler, Rachel Ward.

Contributors:
Andrew Ballard, Terence Brown, Rosie Hanson, Claire Jackson.

With thanks to Peter Caunter and Ceara Hayden for the proofreading.

ISBN: 978 1 84762 981 4

Groovy website: www.cgpbooks.co.uk

Jolly bits of clipart from CorelDRAW®
Printed by Elanders Ltd, Newcastle upon Tyne

Based on the classic CGP style created by Richard Parsons.

How to Use This Book

- Hold the book <u>upright</u>, approximately <u>50 cm</u> from your face, ensuring that the text looks like <u>this</u>, not s̄ı̄ɥ̄ʇ̄. Alternatively, place the book on a <u>horizontal</u> surface (e.g. a table or desk) and sit adjacent to the book, at a distance which doesn't make the text too small to read.

- In case of emergency, press the two halves of the book together <u>firmly</u> in order to close.

- Before attempting to use this book, familiarise yourself with the following <u>safety information</u>:

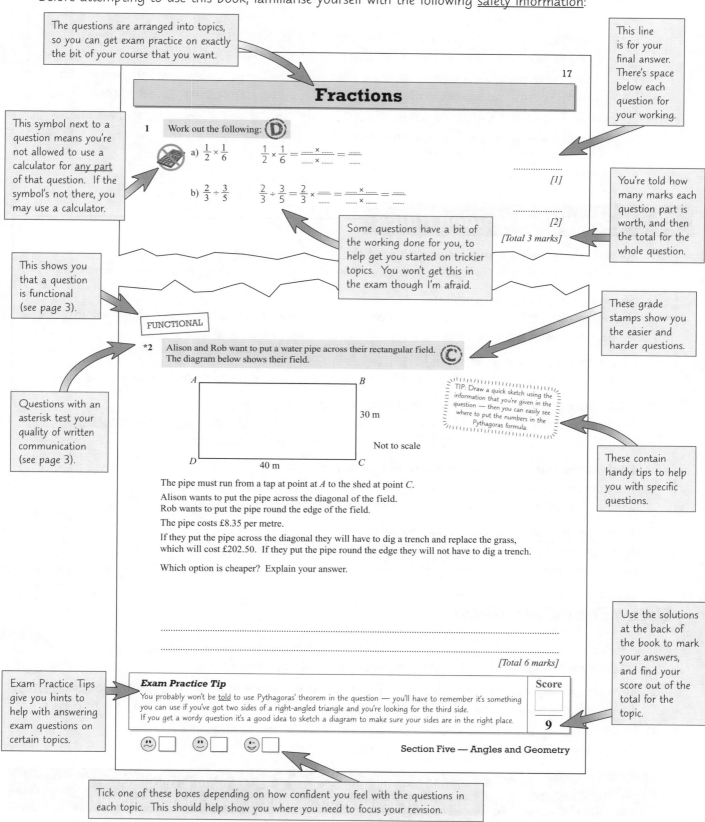

The questions are arranged into topics, so you can get exam practice on exactly the bit of your course that you want.

This line is for your final answer. There's space below each question for your working.

Fractions

17

This symbol next to a question means you're not allowed to use a calculator for <u>any part</u> of that question. If the symbol's not there, you may use a calculator.

1 Work out the following: (D)

a) $\frac{1}{2} \times \frac{1}{6}$ $\qquad$ $\frac{1}{2} \times \frac{1}{6} = \frac{\_\_\_ \times \_\_\_}{\_\_\_ \times \_\_\_} = \frac{\_\_\_}{\_\_\_}$

b) $\frac{2}{3} \div \frac{3}{5}$ $\qquad$ $\frac{2}{3} \div \frac{3}{5} = \frac{2}{3} \times \frac{\_\_\_}{\_\_\_} = \frac{\_\_\_ \times \_\_\_}{\_\_\_ \times \_\_\_} = \frac{\_\_\_}{\_\_\_}$

.... [1]

.... [2]

[Total 3 marks]

You're told how many marks each question part is worth, and then the total for the whole question.

Some questions have a bit of the working done for you, to help get you started on trickier topics. You won't get this in the exam though I'm afraid.

This shows you that a question is functional (see page 3).

FUNCTIONAL

These grade stamps show you the easier and harder questions.

Questions with an asterisk test your quality of written communication (see page 3).

*2 Alison and Rob want to put a water pipe across their rectangular field. (C) The diagram below shows their field.

A ——————— B

30 m

D —— 40 m —— C

Not to scale

TIP: Draw a quick sketch using the information that you're given in the question — then you can easily see where to put the numbers in the Pythagoras formula.

These contain handy tips to help you with specific questions.

The pipe must run from a tap at point at A to the shed at point C.

Alison wants to put the pipe across the diagonal of the field.
Rob wants to put the pipe round the edge of the field.

The pipe costs £8.35 per metre.

If they put the pipe across the diagonal they will have to dig a trench and replace the grass, which will cost £202.50. If they put the pipe round the edge they will not have to dig a trench.

Which option is cheaper? Explain your answer.

....

....

[Total 6 marks]

Use the solutions at the back of the book to mark your answers, and find your score out of the total for the topic.

Exam Practice Tip
You probably won't be <u>told</u> to use Pythagoras' theorem in the question — you'll have to remember it's something you can use if you've got two sides of a right-angled triangle and you're looking for the third side. If you get a wordy question it's a good idea to sketch a diagram to make sure your sides are in the right place.

Score

9

Exam Practice Tips give you hints to help with answering exam questions on certain topics.

☹ ☐ ☺ ☐ ☺ ☐

Section Five — Angles and Geometry

Tick one of these boxes depending on how confident you feel with the questions in each topic. This should help show you where you need to focus your revision.

Exam Tips

WJEC Exam Stuff

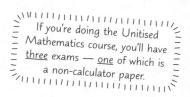

If you're doing the Unitised Mathematics course, you'll have <u>three</u> exams — <u>one</u> of which is a non-calculator paper.

1) You'll have <u>two</u> exams — one <u>calculator</u> exam and one <u>non-calculator</u> exam.

2) Both exams are <u>1 hr 45 mins</u> long and both are worth <u>100 marks</u>.

3) Timings in the exam are really important, so here's a quick guide...

- As each paper is worth <u>100 marks</u> and you've got <u>105 minutes</u> to complete the paper, you should spend about a <u>minute per mark</u> working on each question (i.e. 2 marks = 2 mins).

- That'll leave you with <u>5 minutes</u> at the end of the exam to <u>check</u> back through your answers and make sure you haven't made any silly mistakes. <u>Not</u> to just stare at that hottie in front.

- If you're totally, hopelessly stuck on a question, just <u>leave it</u> and <u>move on</u> to the next one. You can always <u>go back</u> to it at the end if you've got enough time.

There are a Few Golden Rules

1) **Always, always, always make sure you <u>read the question properly</u>.**
   For example, if the question asks you to give your answer in metres, <u>don't</u> give it in centimetres.

2) **Show <u>each step</u> in your <u>working</u>.**
   You're less likely to make a mistake if you write things out in stages. And even if your final answer's wrong, you'll probably pick up <u>some marks</u> if the examiner can see that your <u>method</u> is right.

3) **Check that your answer is <u>sensible</u>.**
   Worked out an angle of 450° or 0.045° in a triangle? You've probably gone wrong somewhere...

4) **Make sure you give your answer to the right <u>degree of accuracy</u>.**
   The question might ask you to round to a certain number of <u>significant figures</u> or <u>decimal places</u>. So make sure you do just that, otherwise you'll almost certainly lose marks.

5) **Look at the number of <u>marks</u> a question is worth.**
   If a question's worth 2 or more marks, you're not going to get them all for just writing down the final answer — you're going to have to <u>show your working</u>.

6) **Write your answers as <u>clearly</u> as you can.**
   If the examiner can't read your answer you won't get any marks, even if it's right.

Obeying these Golden Rules will help you get as many marks as you can in the exam — but they're no use if you haven't learnt the stuff in the first place. So make sure you revise well and do <u>as many</u> practice questions as you can.

Using Your Calculator

1) Your calculator can make questions a lot easier for you, but only if you <u>know how to use it</u>. Make sure you know what the different buttons do and how to use them.

2) If you're working out a <u>big calculation</u> on your calculator, it's best to do it in <u>stages</u> and use the <u>memory</u> to store the answers to the different parts. If you try and do it all in one go, it's too easy to mess it up.

3) If you're feeling reckless, and decide to do a question all in one go on your calculator, use <u>brackets</u> so the calculator knows which bits to do first.

REMEMBER: <u>Golden Rule number 2</u> still applies, even if you're using a calculator — you should still write down <u>all</u> the steps you're doing so the examiner can see the method you're using.

You Need to Understand the Command Words

Command words are the words in a question that tell you what to do.
If you don't know what they mean, you might not be able to answer the questions properly.

Calculate...   This means you'll have to work something out — either using pen and paper OR your calculator.

Work out...   This is a bit like 'calculate', except you might be able to do the sum in your head.

Find...   You'll have to use a mixture of problem-solving skills and maths to find the answer to a question. It might not be immediately obvious what calculation you have to do.

Explain...   You have to use words to give reasons for something.

Show that...   You have to use maths to show that something is true.

> With 'explain' and 'show that' questions, the number of marks available can give you an idea of how much you need to write.

Functional Questions

> On Foundation Tier papers, 30-40% of the total marks available are from functional questions.

Some of the questions in your exams will be wordy questions about a real-life situation.

These are called functional questions. Functional questions are a bit trickier than normal questions because you have to work out what you are being asked to do. Here are some useful steps to follow:

1) Read the question carefully so you can work out what maths you need to use.

2) Underline the information that you need to answer the question — you won't always have to use all of the numbers they give you.

3) Write the question out in maths and then answer it, showing your working as usual.

In this book, questions which contain functional elements are marked with this stamp: | **FUNCTIONAL** |

Your exam paper won't mark them up though, so try to get used to how these questions look, so that you can spot them in your exam.

Quality of Written Communication

> This may seem daft when it's a maths exam, but if the examiner doesn't think you've communicated your answer well enough, you'll lose marks.

Some questions in the exams will tell you that you'll be assessed on your quality of written communication. This means you'll be tested on your ability to explain things clearly, as well as your ability to do good maths. When you're answering questions like this, make sure you...

- Use your neatest handwriting so the examiner can easily read your answer.
- Check that your spelling, punctuation and grammar are ~~rigit rihgt~~ correct.
- Show every step of your working, and lay it out in a clear and coherent way.
- Use specialist vocabulary if you need to.

(You should already be doing all these things in every answer anyway, so they're really nothing to worry about...)

Ordering Numbers and Place Value

1 Use the number lines to answer the following questions.

a) Write down the number shown by the arrow below. Ⓖ

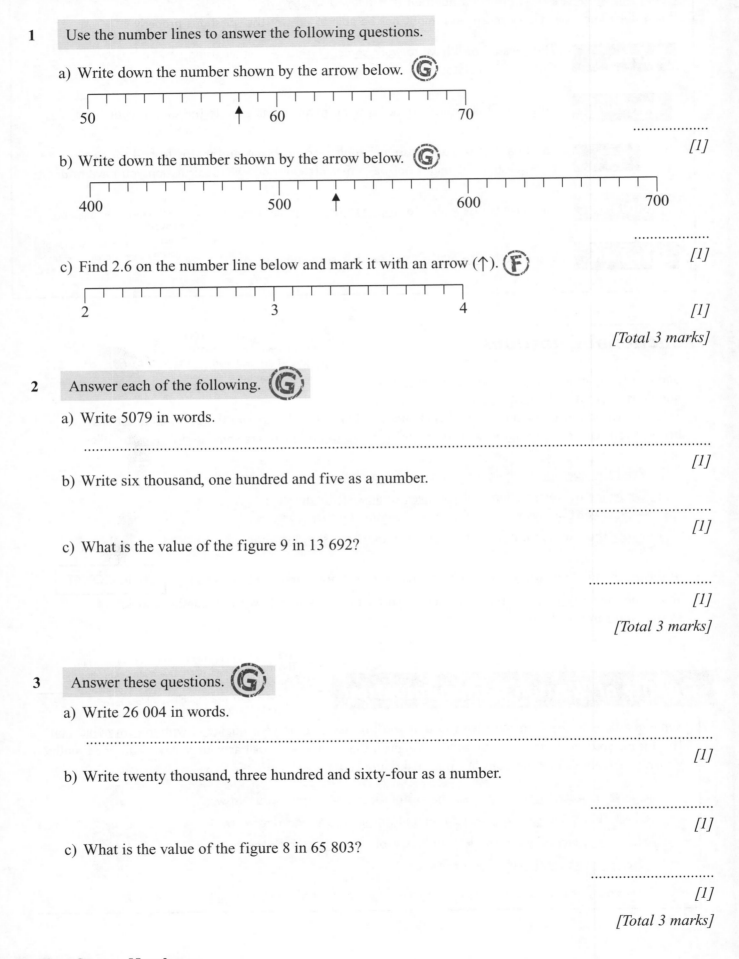

.... [1]

b) Write down the number shown by the arrow below. Ⓖ

.... [1]

c) Find 2.6 on the number line below and mark it with an arrow (↑). Ⓕ

[1]

[Total 3 marks]

2 Answer each of the following. Ⓖ

a) Write 5079 in words.

.... [1]

b) Write six thousand, one hundred and five as a number.

.... [1]

c) What is the value of the figure 9 in 13 692?

.... [1]

[Total 3 marks]

3 Answer these questions. Ⓖ

a) Write 26 004 in words.

.... [1]

b) Write twenty thousand, three hundred and sixty-four as a number.

.... [1]

c) What is the value of the figure 8 in 65 803?

.... [1]

[Total 3 marks]

4   Answer the following questions. (G)

a) Write 420 457 in words.

....

[1]

b) Write six million as a number.

....

[1]

c) Write down the value of the figure 2 in 102 487

....

[1]

[Total 3 marks]

5   The mileages of four cars are given below.   Put the distances in order, starting with the lowest. (F)

98 653   100 003   98 649   100 010

.... , ... , ... , ...

[Total 1 mark]

6   Put these numbers in order of size, from high to low. (F)

53.3   35.6   35.54   52.91   35.06

.... , ... , ... , ... , ...

[Total 1 mark]

7   Anne has five cards, each with a number written on. (G)

| 4 | 7 | 1 | 8 | 2 |

She lines up all the cards to make a 5 digit number.

a) What is the smallest number she can make?

....

[1]

b) What is the largest number she can make?

....

[1]

[Total 2 marks]

Score:

16

Section One — Numbers

Addition and Subtraction

1 Jamie has 522 stickers. He gives 197 to his brother and 24 to his sister. How many stickers does he have left?

....
[Total 2 marks]

FUNCTIONAL

2 Maci's car has failed its MOT. Using the information below, calculate the total cost of all the repairs.

MOT Results

FAILED

FAIL

Areas for attention:
- Exhaust — need full replacement
- Brakes — need new disc and pad on one wheel
- Tyres — tread depth too low on all tyres, need to replace all four

Price List	(includes labour costs and VAT)		
Tyres		**Exhaust**	
Each:	£28	Part Replacement:	£140
Pair:	£50	Full Replacement:	£290
Full Set:	£95		
		Maintenance	
Brakes		Oil Change:	£49
Pads (each):	£39	Adjust Tracking:	£62
Discs (each):	£59	AirCon Recharge:	£55
		Suspension Coil:	£98

£ ....
[Total 3 marks]

3 Eric goes to town with £15. He spends £8.50 on a new scarf.
He meets his nan who gives him £20 and tells him to take £10 of it home for his sister.
Eric then sees a jumper he likes which costs £18.

 If Eric buys the jumper, will he still have £10 to give to his sister?
Show how you worked out your answer.

[Total 2 marks]

Section One — Numbers

4 Find the value of 17.3 – 5.54

....
[Total 1 mark]

FUNCTIONAL

5 Sue and Alan meet Mark in a juice bar.
Mark offers to buy a round of drinks.

 Mark wants a Passion Fruit Punch and
Sue and Alan both want a Tutti Frutti.

Mark pays with a £10 note.
How much change will he get?

Juice Bar Price List	
St Clements:	£2.80
Cranberry Crush:	£2.90
Tutti Frutti:	£2.40
Passion Fruit Punch:	£2.15

£ ....
[Total 2 marks]

FUNCTIONAL

6 Zayn stops at a café for breakfast.

New Road Café

Breakfast Snacks:		Drinks:	
Toast (2 slices)	£1.50	Tea	£1.40
Yoghurt with fruit	£1.90	Coffee	£1.50
Raisin bagel	£2.30	Fresh orange juice	£1.80

Breakfast deal of the day:
Raisin bagel & fresh orange juice   £3.40

Zayn buys 2 raisin bagels, a tea, a coffee and a fresh orange juice.
He pays the lowest possible price.

If he pays with a £10 note, how much change will he get?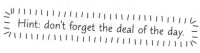

Hint: don't forget the deal of the day.

£ ....
[Total 3 marks]

Score: ☐

13

Multiplying and Dividing Without a Calculator

1 Work out:

 a) 113×76

....
[2]

b) 376×48

....
[2]

[Total 4 marks]

2 Work out:

 a) $19 + 26 \div 2$

....
[2]

b) $(22 - 18) \times (3 + 8)$

Remember the rules for BODMAS.

....
[2]

[Total 4 marks]

FUNCTIONAL

3 Georgie is a sales representative. She drives to different companies to sell air conditioning units.

 When she has to travel, her employer pays fuel expenses of 30p per mile. She drives to a job in the morning and drives home again later that day. She is also given £8 to cover any food expenses for each day that she is not in the office.

The distances to her jobs for this week are shown on the right.

Find Georgie's total expenses for this week.

Hint: think carefully about the total distance travelled.

This Week:

Mon — Buckshaw, 30 miles
Tues — in office
Weds — Wortham, 28 miles
Thurs — Harborough, 39 miles
Fri — Scotby, 40 miles

£ ....
[Total 5 marks]

4 Daffodils cost £1.85 per bunch.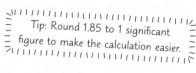

How many bunches of daffodils can be bought for £10?

Number of bunches $= \dfrac{10}{1.85} \approx \dfrac{10}{......} = $ ....

Tip: Round 1.85 to 1 significant figure to make the calculation easier.

.... bunches

[Total 2 marks]

5 Alanna buys 15 tickets for a concert for her and some friends. Each ticket is the same price. She pays with £200 and gets £5 change.

How much does each ticket cost?

£ ....

[Total 3 marks]

FUNCTIONAL

6 James is having a party. He has worked out how much food he needs to buy per person and goes to the shop to buy the things that he needs.

Crisps come in 300 g packets.

There are 8 slices per pizza.

James is expecting there to be 15 people, including himself, at the party.

> For each person:
> • 3 slices of pizza
> • 25 g of crisps

How many pizzas and how many packets of crisps does he need to buy?

.... pizzas

.... packets of crisps

[Total 5 marks]

Exam Practice Tip

It's always important to show your working, but it's especially important for these non-calculator questions — because they all include marks for using a correct method. If you don't show your working, you'll be throwing away valuable marks in the exam.

Score

23

Section One — Numbers

Multiplying and Dividing with Decimals

1 Give your answers to the following, without using a calculator:

 a) 16×0.7

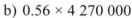
Hint: try working out 16 × 7 first.

b) 25×1.9

....
[2]

....
[2]
[Total 4 marks]

2 Given that $56 \times 427 = 23\ 912$, find the value of:

a) 5.6×4.27

....
[1]

b) $0.56 \times 4\ 270\ 000$

....
[1]

c) $2391.2 \div 4.27$

....
[1]
[Total 3 marks]

3 Work out 0.7×0.8

....
[Total 2 marks]

4 Work out the value of each of the following:

a) $14 \div 0.7$

$$14 \div 0.7 = \frac{14}{0.7} = \frac{\ldots}{7} = \ldots$$

....
[2]

b) $23 \div 0.46$

....
[2]
[Total 4 marks]

Score:
13

Negative Numbers

1 Put the numbers below in order from lowest to highest.

−102.4   98.9   −102.7   99.5   −99.8   −98.9   −103.1

.... , ... , ... , ... , ... , ... , ...

[Total 1 mark]

2 The table below shows the minimum and maximum temperatures in four cities one day in January.

City	Min. temperature (°C)	Max. temperature (°C)
London	4	9
Paris	7	11
St Petersburg	−8	−2
Christchurch	16	22

a) What was the difference between the maximum and minimum temperatures in London?

.... °C

[1]

b) Which city had the **lowest** minimum temperature?

....

[1]

c) What was the difference in temperature between the highest maximum temperature and the lowest minimum temperature across the four cities?

.... °C

[3]

[Total 5 marks]

3 Work out:

a) −11 × 7

....

[1]

b) −72 ÷ −8

....

[1]

[Total 2 marks]

Score:

8

Special Types of Number

1 Choose a number from the list which matches each description.

> 12   100   32   41   27   15   50

a) An odd number bigger than 30.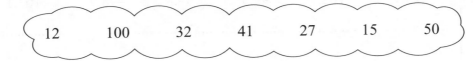

....

[1]

b) A square number.

....

[1]

c) A cube number.

....

[1]

[Total 3 marks]

2 Write down the value of each of the following:

   a) 9^2

....

[1]

b) 4^3

....

[1]

c) $\sqrt{36}$

....

[1]

[Total 3 marks]

Score:

6

Section One — Numbers

Prime Numbers, Multiples and Factors

1 Look at the list of numbers below.

1   7   11   12   15   21

a) Write down a number from the list which is a prime number.

....

[1]

b) Which number in the list is a multiple of 5?

....

[1]

c) Write down a number from the list which is a factor of 30 and is greater than 5.

....

[1]

d) Write down two numbers from the list whose sum is a prime number.

.... and ....

[1]

[Total 4 marks]

2 Write down:

a) **all** the factors of 20,

....

[2]

b) all the multiples of 8 which appear in the list below.

55 56 57 58   59 60 61 62 63 64 65

....

[1]

[Total 3 marks]

3 Write down:

a) two multiples of 21,

.... , ...

[1]

b) a prime number between 45 and 50.

....

[1]

[Total 2 marks]

Score:

9

Section One — Numbers

Prime Factors, LCM and HCF

1 Find:

a) 72 as a product of its prime factors. Give your answer in index form.

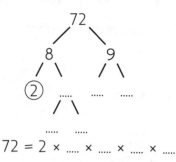

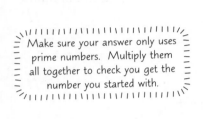
Make sure your answer only uses prime numbers. Multiply them all together to check you get the number you started with.

$72 = 2 \times \underline{\quad} \times \underline{\quad} \times \underline{\quad} \times \underline{\quad}$

....

[3]

b) the highest common factor (HCF) of 54 and 72.

....

[1]

[Total 4 marks]

2 The number 132 can be written as $2^2 \times 3 \times 11$.
Using this information, find the highest common factor (HCF) of 132 and 84.

Hint — first write 84 as a product of its prime factors.

....

[Total 3 marks]

FUNCTIONAL

3 Phil is making jam.

He needs to buy mini jam jars which come in packs of 35 and lids which come in packs of 55. He doesn't want to have any jars or lids left over.

What is the minimum number of packs of jars he needs to buy?

Multiples of 35 are: 35, 70, ..., ..., ..., ..., ..., ..., ..., ..., ..., ...
Multiples of 55 are: 55, 110, ..., ..., ..., ..., ..., ...

So the LCM is ...., which is the minimum number of jars he needs.
So the minimum number of packs he needs is .... ÷ .... = ... packs

....

[Total 3 marks]

Score: ⬜

10

Fractions, Decimals and Percentages

1 Convert each of the following: (E)

a) $\frac{3}{4}$ to a decimal.

....
[1]

b) 0.06 to a percentage.

....
[1]

c) 35% to a fraction in its simplest form.

....
[2]

[Total 4 marks]

2 Mary and Sam both sat a maths test and were given a mark out of 20. (E)

Mary scored $\frac{14}{20}$.

a) Convert her score to a percentage.

.... %
[2]

Sam got 85% on the test.

b) What was Sam's mark out of 20 as a fraction?

....
[2]

[Total 4 marks]

3 Write down the following: (E)

a) 80% as a decimal.

....
[1]

b) $\frac{5}{8}$ as a decimal.

....
[1]

c) $\frac{5}{8}$, 80% and 0.65 in ascending order.

.... , ..., ...
[1]

[Total 3 marks]

Score: ☐

11

Equivalent Fractions

1 Answer the following questions.

 a) Write the fraction $\frac{12}{30}$ in its simplest form.

....
[1]

b) Find the fraction of the shape below which is shaded.
Write this fraction in its simplest form.

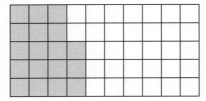

....
[2]

c) Shade $\frac{4}{5}$ of the shape to the right.

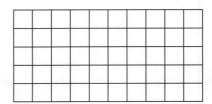

[1]

[Total 4 marks]

2 Convert each of the following:

 a) $\frac{18}{7}$ to a mixed number.

....
[1]

b) $1\frac{3}{4}$ to an improper fraction.

....
[1]

[Total 2 marks]

3 Use the lists of fractions below to answer the following questions.

a) Give the **two** fractions from the list below that are not equivalent to $\frac{1}{3}$

$\frac{3}{9}$ $\frac{2}{6}$ $\frac{3}{12}$ $\frac{5}{15}$ $\frac{6}{20}$ $\frac{8}{24}$

....
[2]

b) Which fraction in the following list is the largest?

$\frac{4}{5}$ $\frac{7}{9}$ $\frac{13}{15}$

You must show your working.

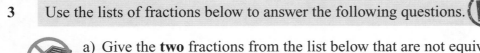

$\frac{4}{5} = \frac{.....}{45}$ $\frac{7}{9} = \frac{.....}{.....}$ $\frac{13}{15} = \frac{.....}{.....}$

....
[3]

[Total 5 marks]

Score:

11

Fractions

1 Work out the following:

 a) $\frac{1}{2} \times \frac{1}{6}$ $\frac{1}{2} \times \frac{1}{6} = \frac{...... \times ......}{...... \times ......} = \frac{......}{......}$

....

[1]

b) $\frac{2}{3} \div \frac{3}{5}$ $\frac{2}{3} \div \frac{3}{5} = \frac{2}{3} \times \frac{......}{......} = \frac{...... \times ......}{...... \times ......} = \frac{......}{......}$

....

[2]

[Total 3 marks]

2 Find the following:

 a) $\frac{3}{4} \times \frac{2}{5}$, giving your answer in its simplest form.

....

[2]

b) $\frac{2}{9}$ as a decimal.

$$9\overline{)2.000...}$$

....

[3]

[Total 5 marks]

3 Find the following:

 a) $\frac{1}{6} + \frac{2}{3}$ $\frac{1}{6} + \frac{2}{3} = \frac{1}{6} + \frac{......}{6} = \frac{...... + ...}{......} = \frac{......}{......}$

....

[2]

b) $\frac{7}{8} - \frac{3}{4}$ $\frac{7}{8} - \frac{3}{4} = \frac{7}{8} - \frac{......}{8} = \frac{...... - ......}{......} = \frac{......}{......}$

....

[2]

[Total 4 marks]

4 Work out the following. Write your answers in their simplest form.

 a) $\frac{1}{3} + \frac{2}{5}$ *Make sure each fraction has the same denominator before you try to add them.*

....

[2]

b) $\frac{1}{2} - \frac{2}{7}$

....

[2]

[Total 4 marks]

Section One — Numbers

18

5 Find: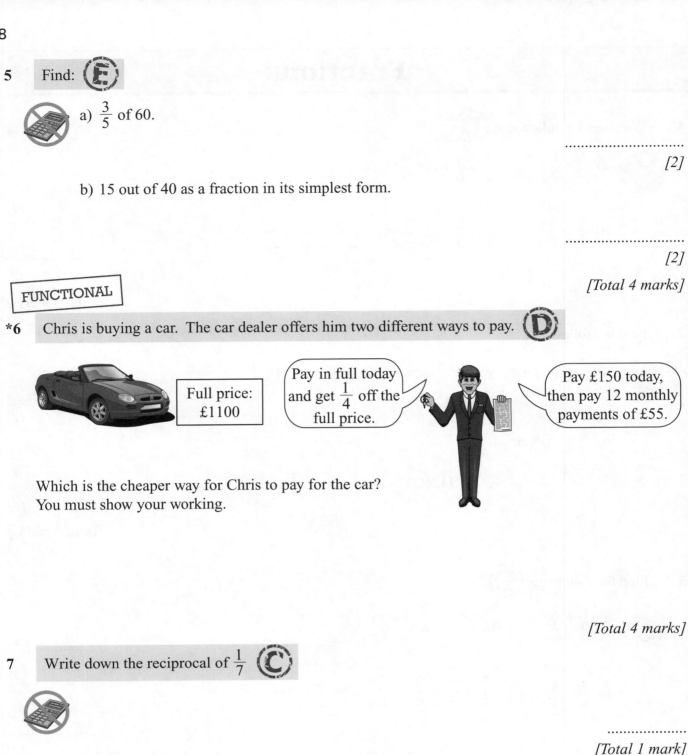

a) $\frac{3}{5}$ of 60.

....

[2]

b) 15 out of 40 as a fraction in its simplest form.

....

[2]

[Total 4 marks]

FUNCTIONAL

*6 Chris is buying a car. The car dealer offers him two different ways to pay. **D**

Full price: £1100

Pay in full today and get $\frac{1}{4}$ off the full price.

Pay £150 today, then pay 12 monthly payments of £55.

Which is the cheaper way for Chris to pay for the car?
You must show your working.

[Total 4 marks]

7 Write down the reciprocal of $\frac{1}{7}$ **C**

....

[Total 1 mark]

8 Sarah is ordering pizza for her birthday party. **C**

There will be 12 people in total at her party.
Sarah wants to order enough so that each person can have $\frac{2}{5}$ of a pizza.
How many pizzas should she order?

....

[Total 3 marks]

Score:

28

Section One — Numbers

Proportion Problems

1   Brown sauce can be bought in three different sizes. The price of each is shown on the right. Which size of bottle is the best value for money?

250 ml £2.30

330 ml £2.97

500 ml £4.10

.... ml

[Total 2 marks]

2   Cat is baking some muffins for an event in her village hall. The list of ingredients below will make 20 muffins.

> ### Ingredients
> **175 g** flour (plain)
> **175 g** butter
> **120 g** sugar
> **2½ tsp** baking powder
> **4** eggs (medium)

Cat wants to make enough muffins for 70 people.

Work out how much she will need of each ingredient.

Flour: (175 ÷ 20) × 70 = ... g

Butter: (............ ÷ 20) × 70 = ... g

Sugar: (............ ÷ ....) × .... = ... g

Baking powder: (............ ÷ ....) × .... = ... tsp

Eggs: (............ ÷ ....) × .... = ...

Flour: .... g

Butter: .... g

Sugar: .... g

Baking powder: .... tsp

Eggs: ....

[Total 3 marks]

Section One — Numbers

*3   Heston bought 8.6 kg of broccoli and 13 tins of custard powder for £46.71. (D)

The broccoli cost £1.35 per kg.
How much did each tin of custard powder cost?

£ ....
[Total 4 marks]

4   Christina is travelling to Andorra to go skiing. (D)

a) She changed £275 into euros (€) before leaving the UK. The exchange rate was £1 = €1.15.
How many euros did she receive?

€ ....
[2]

b) After returning to the UK, Christina still has €120 left over. The exchange rate is now £1 = €1.25.
How many pounds will she get if she changes half of her euros back?

£ ....
[2]
[Total 4 marks]

5   Isambard is the manager of a construction firm. (D)

He knows that it will take a team of 25 men 48 hours in total to build a section of a bridge.
How many hours will it take a team of 16 men to build the same section?

.... hours
[Total 4 marks]

Exam Practice Tip

Proportion is really just all about multiplying and dividing — in general, it's quite likely that you can answer questions on proportion (like the ones on these pages) by finding the amount/cost for "one thing" and then either using this to compare the different options, or multiplying it by the number of things you need.

Score

17

Percentages

1 Find 60% of £450.

£ ....
[Total 2 marks]

2 A farmer has 50 pigs. 35 are female.

  What percentage of the pigs are male?

....
[Total 3 marks]

3 Aled wants to buy a suitcase to take on holiday.

He sees a suitcase which was £18, but today it has 10% off.
a) How much money would he get off the suitcase if he bought it today?

£ ....
[2]

He sees another suitcase which was originally £24, but has been reduced to £18.
b) What is the percentage discount on this suitcase?

.... %
[2]

[Total 4 marks]

4 Jamila puts £200 into a bank account which earns her 3% simple interest per annum.
How much interest will she have earned after 4 years?

3% = 3 ÷ .... = ...

3% of £200 = ... × £200 = £ ....

Interest after 4 years = ... × £ .... = £ ....

£ ....
[Total 3 marks]

Section One — Numbers

5　Jane owns a fashion shop.

Jane sells a pair of jeans for £33.25 plus VAT at 20%.
a) How much does she sell the pair of jeans for? **(D)**

£ ....
[3]

A new style of dress arrives for her to sell.
If she sells each dress for £29, she will make a profit of £6.38 per dress.
b) Calculate the profit as a percentage of the sale price. **(C)**

.... %
[2]

Jane bought a range of necklaces last year for £200, but only sold them for a total of £175.
c) Work out Jane's loss on the range of necklaces as a percentage. **(C)**

.... %
[3]
[Total 8 marks]

FUNCTIONAL

6　Francis is buying a new computer from an electrical store. **(C)**

The store offers two ways of paying for the computer:

CASH PRICE
£750

HIRE PURCHASE
12% of cash price as a deposit,
plus 18 monthly payments of £44

How much would it cost Francis in total to buy the computer through the hire purchase scheme?

£ ....
[Total 3 marks]

7　A new house cost £120 000, but increased in value by 15% each year. **(C)**

Work out its value after 5 years, to the nearest £1000.

£ ....
[Total 3 marks]

8 Liam has just got a new job as a climbing instructor, with a yearly salary of £16 000. Use the table below to calculate how much tax he will pay each year.

Salary	Income Tax
up to £9440	0% (Tax Free Allowance)
over £9440	20% (on anything above £9440)

£ ....

[Total 3 marks]

9 Jenson buys a new car for £21 500. The value of the car depreciates by 11% each year.

How much will the car be worth after 2 years?

£ ....

[Total 3 marks]

FUNCTIONAL

*10 John buys broken computers, fixes them and then sells them on.

He bought 20 broken computers for £50 each. He then spent £20 fixing each one.
He gave them a selling price so that he made a profit of 40% on the **total** he had spent per computer.
He sold 12 computers at this price.
He then reduced this price by 12% and sold the remaining 8 computers.

How much profit or loss did John make? Show your working clearly.

[Total 8 marks]

Section One — Numbers

Ratios

1 Give the ratio $4:12$ in its simplest form.

....
[Total 1 mark]

2 In a class of 26 children, 12 are boys and 14 are girls.

a) What is the ratio of boys to girls? Give your answer in its simplest form.

....
[1]

b) In another class, the ratio of boys to girls is $2:3$. There are 25 children in the class.
How many girls are there?

....
[2]

[Total 3 marks]

FUNCTIONAL

3 Brian is making a fruit punch. He mixes orange juice, pineapple juice
and lemonade in the ratio $4:3:7$. He makes 700 ml of fruit punch.

What volume of each drink does he use?

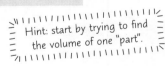
Hint: start by trying to find the volume of one "part".

1 part = 700 ÷ (.......... + ... + ...)

= 700 ÷ ....

= .... ml

Orange juice: .... × 4 = ... ml
Pineapple juice: .... × .... = ... ml
Lemonade: .... × .... = ... ml

Orange juice: .... ml

Pineapple juice: .... ml

Lemonade: .... ml

[Total 3 marks]

4 Andy, Louise and Christine have £160. They share it in the ratio 3 : 6 : 7.

How much money did Christine get?

£ ....

[Total 2 marks]

FUNCTIONAL

5 Brian is feeding his pet budgies, Elmo and Ziggy.

He gives each of his budgies a different feed.
The table shows the proportions of the ingredients in each budgie's feed.

Ingredient	Elmo	Ziggy
Oats	5	8
Sunflower seeds	6	1
Sesame seeds	5	3

A local pet store sells the ingredients.

Brian buys enough ingredients to mix 1600 g of feed for Elmo and 1200 g of feed for Ziggy.

How much do the ingredients cost him in total?

Prices (per kg)

Oats £1.80
Sunflower seeds £6.00
Sesame seeds £4.50

£ ....

[Total 5 marks]

Score:

14

Section One — Numbers

Calculating Bills

1   Leonardo is buying materials from an art shop.
    He buys 4 tubes of red paint, 3 tubes of blue paint, 2 paintbrushes and an easel.

a) Complete his bill for these items.

ITEM	COST
4 tubes of red paint (£1.79 per tube)	
3 tubes of blue paint (£1.99 per tube)	
2 paintbrushes (£7.49 each)	
1 easel	£69.99
TOTAL	

[4]

b) Leonardo has a voucher with him that gives him 20% off all purchases at the store.
   How much money will he save by using the voucher?

£ ....

[1]

[Total 5 marks]

2   Nikola has received a quarterly bill from his electricity supplier.

The first 100 units he uses each quarter cost 12p per unit.
Any electricity he uses above this amount costs 16p per unit.
There is also a fixed quarterly charge of £37.25.

Nikola pays his supplier £135 by direct debit each quarter.
Last quarter he paid his supplier £25 too much, so this will be deducted from his bill this quarter.

Meter reading at the start of the quarter: | 4 | 3 | 2 | 0 | 2 |

Meter reading at the end of the quarter: | 4 | 4 | 4 | 3 | 9 |

How much does Nikola still have to pay?

£ ....

[Total 6 marks]

Score:

11

Section One — Numbers

Rounding Off and Estimating Calculations

1   Round the following to the given degree of accuracy.

a) Josh has 123 people coming to his party. **(F)**
Write this number to the nearest 10.

....
[1]

b) The attendance at a football match was 2568 people. **(F)**
What is this to the nearest hundred?

....
[1]

c) The population of Ulverpool is 452 529. **(E)**
Round this to the nearest 100 000.

....
[1]

[Total 3 marks]

2   The distance between two stars is 428.6237 light years.

a) Round this distance to one decimal place. **(E)**

.... light years
[1]

b) Round this distance to 2 significant figures. **(D)**

.... light years
[1]

[Total 2 marks]

3   Use your calculator to find: **(D)**

$$\frac{4.32^2 - \sqrt{13.4}}{16.3 + 2.19}$$

Give your answer to 3 significant figures.

....
[Total 2 marks]

4   Estimate the value of $\dfrac{12.2 \times 1.86}{0.19}$ **(C)**

> You should start by rounding each number to an easier one.

....
[Total 3 marks]

Score:

10

Powers and Roots

1 Use your calculator to find the following:

a) 8.7^3

....
[1]

b) $\sqrt{2025}$

....
[1]

[Total 2 marks]

2 Estimate the value of $\sqrt{42}$

....
[Total 1 mark]

3 Write as a single power of 6:

   a) $6^4 \times 6^7$

....
[1]

b) $\dfrac{6^5}{6^3}$

....
[1]

[Total 2 marks]

4 Simplify the expression $\dfrac{3^4 \times 3^7}{3^6}$. Leave your answer in index form.

....
[Total 2 marks]

Exam Practice Tip

For some of these questions, you just need to know how to use your calculator to grab some easy marks. Make sure you learn the power rules — if you're multiplying, you add the powers. If you're dividing, you subtract them. Don't forget that the rules ONLY work for powers of the same number (i.e. NOT things like $2^7 \times 3^6$).

Score

7

Section One — Numbers

Simplifying Terms

1 Simplify the following.

a) $p + p + p + p$

....

[1]

b) $m + 3m - 2m$

....

[1]

c) $7r - 2p - 4r + 6p$

....

[2]

[Total 4 marks]

2 Simplify the following.

a) $w \times w \times w \times w \times w$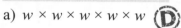

....

[1]

b) $x^9 \div x^3$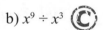

....

[1]

c) $y^2 \times y^3$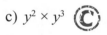

....

[1]

[Total 3 marks]

3 Write the following in their simplest form.

a) $2a \times 5b$

....

[1]

b) $\dfrac{x^8}{x^2 \times x^4}$

....

[2]

c) $(5p^3)^2$

....

[2]

[Total 5 marks]

Score:

12

Multiplying Out Brackets and Common Factors

1 Expand the following.

a) $3(x - 2)$

$$= (3 \times \text{.............}) + (3 \times \text{.............}) = \text{.............} - \text{.............}$$

....
[1]

b) $x(x + 4)$

....
[1]

[Total 2 marks]

2 Multiply out the brackets and simplify where possible.

a) $5(x + y)$

....
[1]

b) $s(2s - 3)$

....
[1]

[Total 2 marks]

3 Expand and simplify $3(x - 1) + 5(x + 2)$.

....
[Total 2 marks]

4 Factorise the following expressions.

a) $6x + 3$

....
[1]

b) $x^2 + 7x$

....
[1]

c) $25p - 15q$

....
[1]

[Total 3 marks]

Exam Practice Tip

In the exam, you can check that you've factorised an expression properly by expanding the brackets back out. You should get the same expression that you started with. If you don't then something must have gone wrong somewhere down the line and you'll need to give it another go. Sorry about that.

Score

9

Solving Equations

1   Solve these equations for x.

    a) $x + 3 = 12$

$x = $ ....
[1]

    b) $6x = 24$

$x = $ ....
[1]

    c) $\frac{x}{5} = 4$

$x = $ ....
[1]

    d) $6 = \frac{42}{x}$

$x = $ ....
[1]

[Total 4 marks]

2   Solve the equations below.

    a) $p - 11 = -7$

$p = $ ....
[1]

    b) $2y - 5 = 9$

$y = $ ....
[2]

    c) $3z + 2 = z + 15$ ⒟

       $3z - z = 15 -$ ....

       $2z =$ ....

       $z =$ .... $\div$ .... $=$ ....

$z = $ ....
[2]

[Total 5 marks]

3   Solve these equations for x.

    a) $3x + 5 = 14$

$x = $ ....
[2]

    b) $7x - 4 = 2x + 1$ ⒟

$x = $ ....
[2]

[Total 4 marks]

4 Solve the following equations.

a) $40 - 3x = 17x$

$x =$ ....

[2]

b) $2y - 5 = 3y - 12$

$y =$ ....

[2]

[Total 4 marks]

5 Find the solution to each of the following equations.

 a) $3(a + 2) = 15$

$(3 \times \text{.........}) + (3 \times \text{.........}) = 15$

$\text{.........} + \text{.........} = 15$

$\text{.........} = \text{.........}$

$a = \text{.........}$

$a =$ ....

[3]

b) $2b - 6 = 2(3b + 1)$

$b =$ ....

[3]

[Total 6 marks]

6 Solve the following equations.

 a) $5(2c - 1) = 4(3c - 2)$

$c =$ ....

[3]

b) $(2p + 14) = \frac{2}{3}(1 - p)$

$p =$ ....

[3]

[Total 6 marks]

Exam Practice Tip

It's a good idea to check your solution by substituting it back into the equation and checking that everything works out properly. It certainly beats sitting and twiddling your thumbs or counting sheep for the last few minutes of your exam.

Score

29

Writing Equations

1 Below is a number machine. (D)

Input

Output

×8 − 5

The output is three times the input.
What is the input?

....
[Total 3 marks]

2 Alexa is playing a number game. (D)

Alexa thinks of a number and divides it by 2. She adds 20 to this new number.
Her answer is equal to 3 times her original number.

What was her original number?

....
[Total 2 marks]

3 The letter *f* represents a number. Write down each of the following in terms of *f*: (D)

a) The number that is twelve less than *f*.

....
[1]

b) The number that is seven more than *f*.

....
[1]

c) The number that is three less than four times *f*.

....
[1]

[Total 3 marks]

4 **X** and **Y** are small metal weights.
Different arrangements of weights can be made to balance, as shown below.

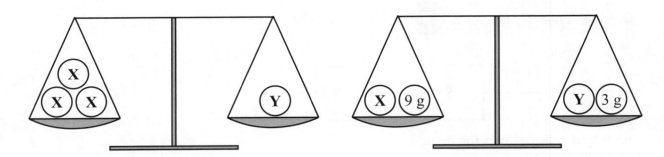

Find the weights of **X** and **Y**.

X = ... g

Y = ... g

[Total 4 marks]

5 *ABC* is a triangle.

Find the size of the largest angle.
Make sure you show all your working.

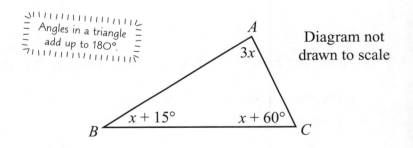

Diagram not
drawn to scale

.....................................°

[Total 4 marks]

Score:

16

Formulas

1 $Q = 7x - 3y$

 Find the value of Q when $x = 8$ and $y = 7$.

....
[Total 2 marks]

2 $S = 4m^2 + 2.5n$

Calculate the value of S when $m = 6.5$ and $n = 4$.

S = (4 × .... × ....) + (2.5 × ....)

S = ... + ...

S = ...
....
[Total 2 marks]

3 The formula for converting a temperature in Celsius (C) to a temperature in Fahrenheit (F) is:

$$F = \frac{9C}{5} + 32$$

Convert 35 °C to Fahrenheit.

.... °F
[Total 2 marks]

FUNCTIONAL

4 The cost of hiring a bouncy castle is calculated using the formula below.

Cost = £7 × Number of hours + Set-up charge

a) How much will it cost to hire a bouncy castle for 13 hours if the set-up charge is £25?

£ ....
[2]

b) The cost of hiring a set of space hoppers is calculated using a different formula:

Cost = (£2 × Number of hours) + (£5 × Number of space hoppers)

How much would it cost to hire 5 space hoppers for 3 hours?

£ ....
[2]

[Total 4 marks]

Section Two — Algebra

5 The cost of hiring a cement mixer is calculated using the following formula: (E)

Cost = £300 + (cost per day × number of days)

How much would Alex have to pay to hire the cement mixer for 3 days if the cost per day is £50?

£.................................

[Total 2 marks]

6 To convert kilometres into miles, Tasmin says that you use the following formula: (E)

Number of miles = (number of kilometres ÷ 8) × 5

Use this to convert 110 kilometres into miles.

.... miles

[Total 2 marks]

7 Rearrange the formula $m = 3p + 4$ into the form $p =$ .... (C)

$p =$ ....

[Total 2 marks]

8 The formula $v = u + at$ can be used to calculate the speed of a car. (C)

a) Rearrange the formula to make u the subject.

....

[1]

b) Rearrange the formula to make t the subject.

....

[2]

[Total 3 marks]

Exam Practice Tip

Remember that a <u>formula</u> is just like an equation — it has an equals sign in it, like 'P = 2x + 3'. An <u>expression</u> doesn't have an equals sign — it's something like '2x + 3'. If you're asked to give a formula in the exam, make sure you give the whole thing and not just an expression, otherwise you won't get all the marks.

Score

19

Number Patterns and Sequences

1 Write down the next two terms in each of the following sequences. (E)

a)   4   12   20   28

.... and ....
[1]

b)   3   7   12   18

.... and ....
[1]

[Total 2 marks]

2 Fill in the gaps in the following sequences, and give the rule for each sequence. (E)

a)   13   18   23   33   ....

Rule: ....
[2]

b)   6   12   24   48   ....

Rule: ....
[2]

[Total 4 marks]

3 A sequence is made of patterns of straight lines and circles. (E)

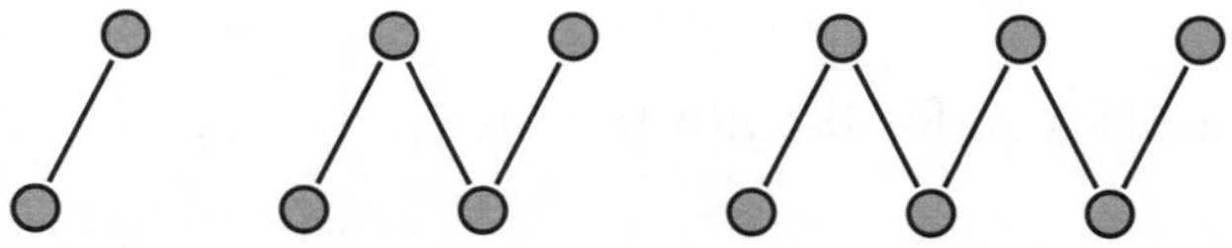

Pattern 1   Pattern 2   Pattern 3

a) Write down the number of circles in Pattern 8.

....
[1]

b) Work out the number of straight lines in the pattern containing 22 circles.

....
[2]

[Total 3 marks]

4 A sequence is made from patterns of triangles. The first three patterns are shown below.

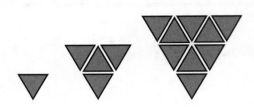

a) Draw the fourth pattern in the sequence.

[1]

b) Find an expression for the number of triangles in the *n*th pattern.

....
[1]

[Total 2 marks]

5 The *n*th term of a sequence is $n^2 + 4$.

a) Find the first term of the sequence.

....
[1]

b) Find the 8th term of the sequence.

....
[1]

[Total 2 marks]

6 The first four terms in a sequence are 2, 9, 16, 23, …

Find the *n*th term of the sequence.

2   9   16   23

....

The common difference is ...., so ....n is in the formula.

n = 1   2   ....
........n = ...
↓   ↓   ↓   ↓   You have to subtract .... to get to the term.
nth term = ...

So the expression for the nth term is ....n − ....

....
[Total 2 marks]

7 This question is about the sequence 3, 7, 11, 15, 19…

Find the *n*th term of the sequence.

....
[Total 2 marks]

Score: ☐
17

Section Two — Algebra

Trial and Improvement

1 The equation $x^3 + 4x = 24$ has a solution between 2 and 3.

Find this solution.
Give your answer correct to 1 decimal place and show all your working.

x	$x^3 + 4x$	
2	$2^3 + (4 \times 2) = 8 + 8 = 16$	Too small
3	$3^3 + (4 \times 3) = \ldots\ldots + \ldots\ldots = \ldots\ldots$	....

$x = $ ....

[Total 4 marks]

2 The equation $x^3 - 2x = 0$ has a solution between 1 and 2.

Find this solution to 1 decimal place.
Use the trial and improvement method and show your working.

$x = $ ....

[Total 4 marks]

Exam Practice Tip

Make sure that you learn the method for solving trial and improvement problems — don't go randomly plugging in numbers all over the place. It's really important that you show all your working — the examiner needs to see that you've been systematic and tried all the values you're supposed to have done.

Score

8

Section Two — Algebra

Inequalities

1 n is an integer. List all the possible values of n that satisfy the inequality $-3 \le n < 2$.

....

[Total 2 marks]

2 Solve the inequality: $2a - 7 \le 11$

....

[Total 2 marks]

3 Solve the following inequalities.

a) $2p > 4$

....

[1]

b) $4q - 5 < 23$

....

[2]

c) $4r - 2 \ge 2r + 5$

....

[2]

[Total 5 marks]

4 Lollipops are sold in packets containing x lollipops.

Alice has 3 packets and 20 extra lollipops.
Emil has 5 packets and 4 extra lollipops.
Emil has more lollipops than Alice.

a) Write an inequality to show this.

....

[1]

b) Solve your inequality.

....

[3]

[Total 4 marks]

Score:

13

Coordinates and Midpoints

1 Two points have been plotted on the grid below. They are labelled **A** and **B**.

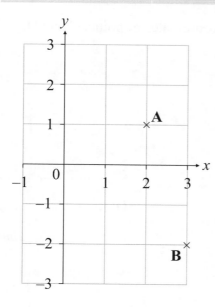

a) Give the coordinates of point **A**.

(.............., ...)
[1]

b) Give the coordinates of point **B**.

(.............., ...)
[1]

c) Point **C** has the coordinates (1, –1).
Mark this point on the grid on the left using a cross (×) and label it **C**.

[1]

[Total 3 marks]

2 Points **Q** and **R** have been plotted on the grid below.

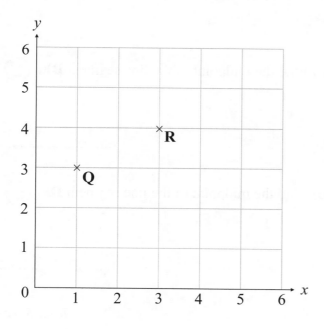

a) What are the coordinates of point **Q**?

(.............., ...)
[1]

b) Point **S** lies on the *x*-axis.
The line **QS** is parallel to the *y*-axis.
What are the coordinates of point **S**?

(.............., ...)
[2]

c) Point **T** lies on the *y*-axis.
The line **TR** is parallel to the *x*-axis.
What are the coordinates of point **T**?

(.............., ...)
[2]

[Total 5 marks]

3   **ABCD** is a parallelogram. Points **A** and **B** have been plotted on the grid below:

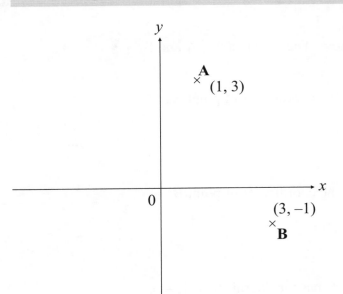

BC and AD are parallel to the *x*-axis.
Point **D** is six units to the left of point **A**.

Give the coordinates of points **C** and **D**.

C: (..............., ...)

D: (..............., ...)

[Total 2 marks]

4   A grid has been drawn below.

a) Plot the points **D** (2, 1), **E** (4, 3) and **F** (6, –3) on this grid.

[1]

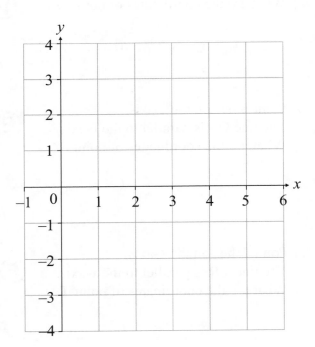

b) Find the midpoint of the line segment **DE**.

(..............., ...)

[2]

c) Find the midpoint of the line segment **DF**.

(..............., ...)

[2]

[Total 5 marks]

Score:

15

Section Three — Graphs

Straight-Line Graphs

1   Use the grid for the questions below.

a) Draw and label the following lines.

$y = 3$

$x = -2$

$y = x$

[3]

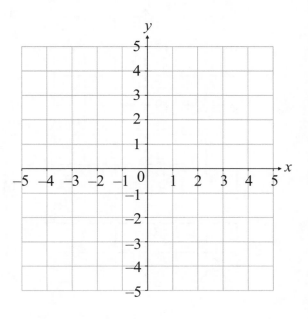

b) What are the coordinates of the point where the lines $y = 3$ and $y = x$ meet?

(................, ...)

[1]

[Total 4 marks]

2   Answer each question below.

a) Complete this table of values for the equation $y = 3x - 2$.

x	-2	-1	0	1	2
y		-5			

[2]

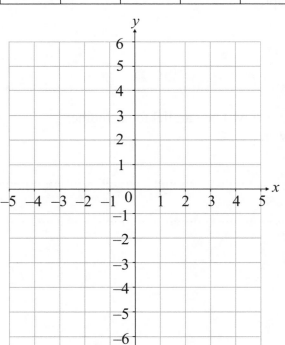

b) Use your table of values to plot the graph of $y = 3x - 2$ on the grid.

[2]

c) On the same grid, plot the graph of $y = -2x + 2$ from $x = -2$ to $x = 2$.

In the exam, you might not always be given a table of values to help you plot a graph — but it's a good idea to draw your own.

[3]

[Total 7 marks]

Section Three — Graphs

3   This is a question about the equation $y = 8 - 3x$.

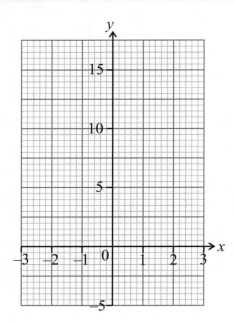

a) Complete this table of values for the equation $y = 8 - 3x$.

x	-2	-1	0	1	2
y				5	

[2]

b) Using the table, draw the graph of $y = 8 - 3x$ on the grid to the left.

[2]

[Total 4 marks]

4   Below are the equations of five graphs.

$y = 3x$ $y = 2x + 6$ $y = x + 6$ $y = 4x - 1$ $y = \frac{1}{2}x + 3$

a) Write down the equation of the steepest graph.

....

[1]

b) Amie says, "the graphs $y = 2x + 6$ and $y = x + 6$ will be parallel to each other".
   Is she correct? Give a reason for your answer.

....

....

[1]

[Total 2 marks]

Exam Practice Tip

When you're drawing straight-line graphs, make sure you always use a ruler — otherwise you'll be throwing away valuable marks in the exam. If one of your points doesn't fit in a straight line with the others, the chances are you've made a mistake filling in your table of values — so it's best to go back and double-check.

Score

17

Travel Graphs

1   The travel graph below shows Selby's bike ride from his
    house (**A**) to the zoo (**C**), which is 25 km away.

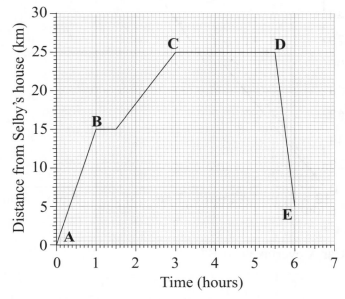

a) After one hour, Selby stops at a bench (**B**) for a rest.
    Find the gradient of the line between point **A** and point **B**.

$$\frac{15 - 0}{\text{......} - \text{......}} = \frac{\text{..........}}{\text{..........}} = \text{..........}$$

    ....
    [2]

b) What does the gradient of the line between point **A** and point **B** represent?

    ....
    [1]

c) How long was Selby's journey to the zoo (**C**) from home (**A**)?

    .... hours
    [1]

d) How long did Selby spend at the zoo?

    .... hours
    [1]

e) After the zoo, Selby stopped at the shops (**E**) for 30 minutes before cycling straight home at a
    constant speed. Given that he arrived home 7 hours after he had first left, complete the graph above.
    [2]

f) How many hours did Selby spend cycling in total during the day?

    .... hours
    [1]

[Total 8 marks]

Section Three — Graphs

2   A group of friends go on holiday. They travel in two cars, Car A
     and Car B.   The journey of each car is shown on the graph below.

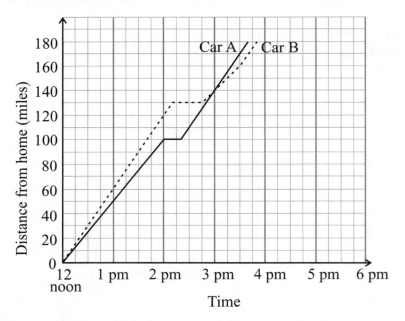

a) At what time does Car A overtake Car B?

....
[1]

b) When Car A stops for a break, how far ahead is Car B?

.... miles
[2]

[Total 3 marks]

3   Edwin drives 120 km home for Christmas. The travel graph shows his journey.

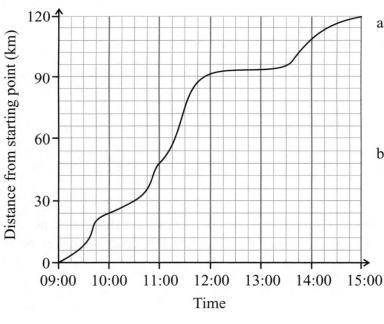

a) What distance did Edwin travel between
    10:00 and 11:00?

.... km
[2]

b) What was his average speed for the
    entire journey?

.... km/h
[2]

[Total 4 marks]

Score: ☐

15

Real-Life Graphs

1 Use the graph to help you answer the questions below.

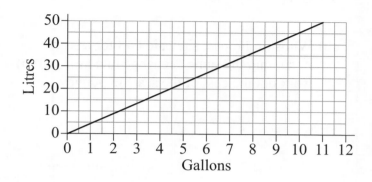

a) A petrol tank holds 8 gallons.
   How many litres is this?

.... litres
   [1]

b) Approximately how many gallons of water
   would fit into a 20 litre container?

.... gallons
   [1]

c) A paddling pool holds 80 litres of water. What is this in gallons? **D**

   40 litres = ... gallons

   40 × .... = 80,

   so, ... gallons × .... = ... gallons

.... gallons
   [3]

   [Total 5 marks]

2 Temperature can be measured in °C and °F.

The table below shows three temperatures in both
degrees Celsius (°C) and degrees Fahrenheit (°F).

Celsius (°C)	10	20	30
Fahrenheit (°F)	50	68	86

a) Plot the points and join them with a straight line to draw
   a conversion graph to change between °C and °F.
   [2]

b) Use your graph to find 26 °C in °F.

.... °F
   [1]

c) Use your graph to find 96 °F in °C.

.... °C
   [1]

   [Total 4 marks]

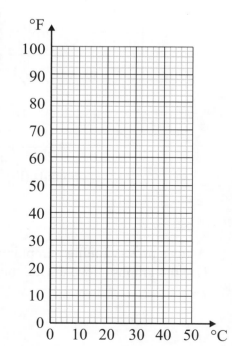

3   Edwige visited France on holiday.

a) She exchanged £180 into euros before leaving the UK. The exchange rate was £1 = €1.25. How many euros did she receive?

€ ....
[2]

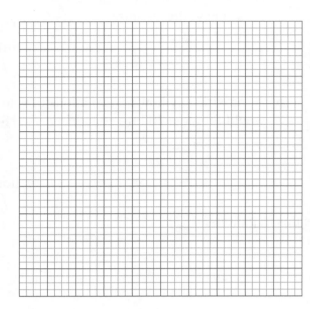

b) Whilst in France, she paid €48 for a scarf. Assuming the same exchange rate as in part a), work out the cost of the scarf in pounds.

£ ....
[2]

c) Using the grid on the left, draw a conversion graph between pounds and euros. Your graph should allow amounts up to €10 to be converted into pounds.

[3]

[Total 7 marks]

4   The graphs below can be used to convert between pounds (lb), kilograms (kg) and stone.

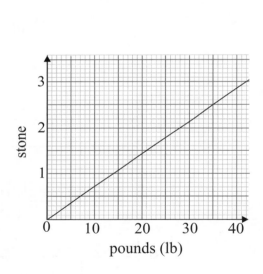

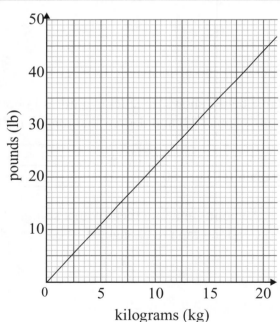

Aston's prize-winning pumpkin weighs 5.5 stone.
Use the graphs above to find the weight of his pumpkin in kilograms.

.... kg
[Total 4 marks]

Score:

20

Section Three — Graphs

Quadratic Graphs

1 A table of values for $y = x^2 - 5$ is shown below.

x	-3	-2	-1	0	1	2
y	4	-1	-4	-5	-4	-1

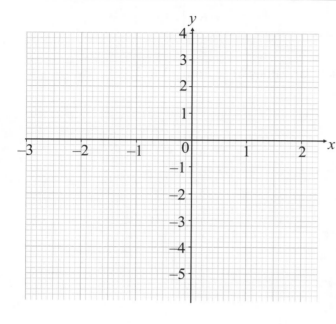

a) Draw the graph of $y = x^2 - 5$ on the grid.

[2]

b) Use your graph to estimate the negative solution to the equation $x^2 - 5 = 0$.
Give your answer to 1 decimal place.

$x =$ ....

[1]

[Total 3 marks]

Don't use a ruler to join up the dots in curved graphs.

2 This question is about the equation $y = x(x + 2)$.

a) Complete the table of values on the right for the equation $y = x(x + 2)$.

x	-4	-3	-2	-1	0	1	2
y	8		0		0	3	8

[1]

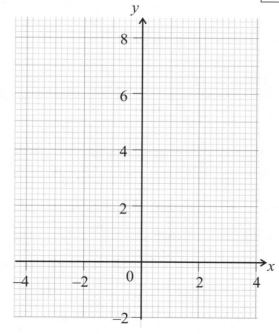

b) On the grid, draw the graph of $y = x(x + 2)$ from $x = -4$ to $x = 2$.

[2]

c) The area of a rectangular paddling pool is 6 m². Given that it is 2 metres longer than it is wide, estimate the width of the paddling pool.

.... m

[2]

[Total 5 marks]

Score:

8

Cubic Graphs

1 This question is about the equation $y = x^3 + 8$.

a) Complete this table of values for the equation $y = x^3 + 8$.

x	-3	-2	-1	0	1	2	3
y		0		8		16	35

[3]

b) On the grid below, draw the graph of $y = x^3 + 8$ for values of x from -3 to 3.

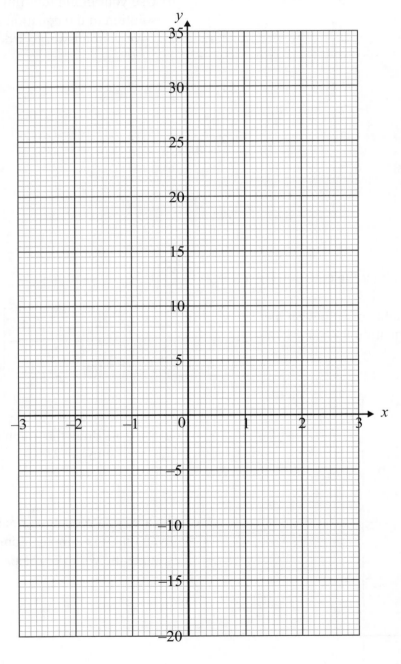

[2]

[Total 5 marks]

Score:

5

Symmetry

1   Below are some incomplete patterns.

a) Shade in four more squares in the grid below so that line AB is a line of symmetry.

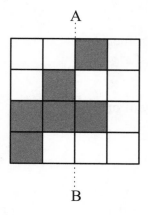

[1]

b) Shade in six more squares so that the grid below has exactly two lines of symmetry.

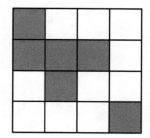

[1]

c) A pattern has been drawn in one section of the grid below.

Draw a pattern in each of the remaining three sections so that the completed pattern has rotational symmetry of order 4 around point **A**.

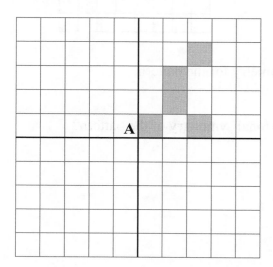

[3]

[Total 5 marks]

2   Each shape below is made with five small squares.   (F)

A   B   C   D   E

a) Two of the shapes have one line of symmetry.
   Write down the letters of these shapes.   .... and ....
                                                                                    [2]

b) Which shape has rotational symmetry of order 2?

                                                                               ....
                                                                                    [1]

Shape D is redrawn on the right.

c) Add one more square to the diagram so that
   shape D has rotational symmetry of order **2**.

                                                                                    [1]

                                                                          [Total 4 marks]

3   Below is a pattern made by shading part of a square grid.   (F)

a) Draw all the lines of symmetry for the pattern.

                                                                                    [2]

b) What is the order of rotational symmetry of the pattern?

                                                                          ....
                                                                                    [1]

                                                                          [Total 3 marks]

Score:

12

Section Four — Shapes and Area

Properties of 2D Shapes

1 Below are four shapes.

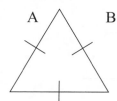 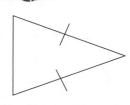 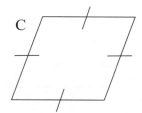 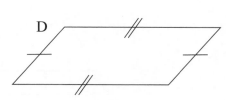

a) What is the mathematical name of shape B?

....

[1]

b) Which of these shapes is a rhombus? Write down the letter.

....

[1]

[Total 2 marks]

2 Draw a quadrilateral that has 2 pairs of equal sides and 2 pairs of equal angles.

[Total 2 marks]

3 Draw a trapezium on the grid below.

[Total 1 mark]

4 Below is a parallelogram.

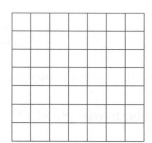

a) How many lines of symmetry does a parallelogram have?

....

[1]

b) What order of rotational symmetry does a parallelogram have?

....

[1]

[Total 2 marks]

Score: ☐

7

Section Four — Shapes and Area

Congruence and Similarity

1   Look at the shapes below.

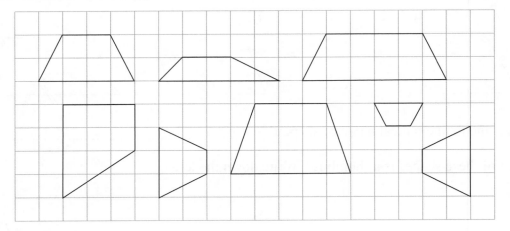

    a) Write C in the two shapes that are **congruent**.   *[1]*

    b) Write S in the two shapes that are **similar**.   *[1]*

[Total 2 marks]

2   The shape below has been divided into triangles.

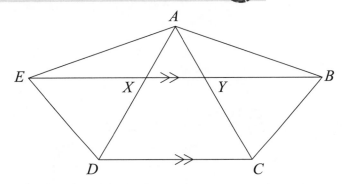

    a) Which triangle in this diagram is congruent to triangle *ABY*?

                                                            ....

                                                            [1]

    b) Which triangle is similar to triangle *ACD*?

                                                            ....

                                                            [1]

[Total 2 marks]

3   Write down the letters of 2 different pairs of congruent shapes.

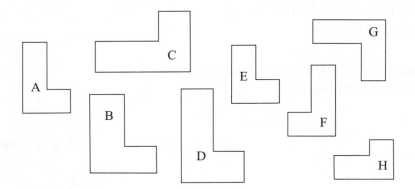

                                      .... and ....

                                        .... and ....

[Total 2 marks]

Score:

6

3D Shapes

1   Write down the mathematical names of the 3D shapes below.

A ....
                                                    [1]

B ....
                                                    [1]

[Total 2 marks]

2   Thomas is making toffee for Christmas presents.

He wants to make boxes to put his toffee in.
He works out that he needs a cuboid as
shown on the right.

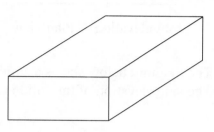

How many of the following does the cuboid have?

a) Faces

                                    ....
                                                    [1]

b) Edges

                                    ....
                                                    [1]

c) Vertices

                                    ....
                                                    [1]

[Total 3 marks]

3   Below are four 3D shapes.

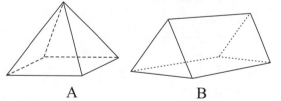 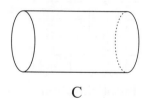 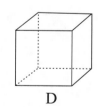

            A   B   C   D

a) What is the name of shape A?

                    ....
                                                    [1]

b) How many faces does shape D have?

                                    ....
                                                    [1]

c) Which shape has 9 edges?

                                    ....
                                                    [1]

d) Which shape has the most vertices?

                                    ....
                                                    [1]

[Total 4 marks]

Score:

9

Section Four — Shapes and Area

Projections

1 The diagram below shows the front elevation and plan view of a house.

Draw the side elevation of the house.

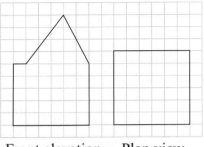

Front elevation   Plan view

Side elevation

[Total 3 marks]

2 The diagram below shows a solid made from identical cubes.
The side elevation of the solid is drawn on the adjacent grid.

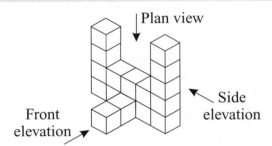

Front elevation   Side elevation

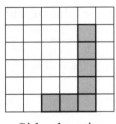

Side elevation

On the grids below, draw the front elevation and plan view of the solid.

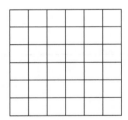

Front elevation

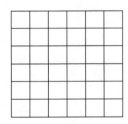

Plan view

[Total 4 marks]

3 The diagram below shows the plan, the front elevation and the side elevation of a prism.

Plan view

Draw a sketch of the solid prism on the grid below.

Front elevation   Side elevation

[Total 2 marks]

Score:

9

Section Four — Shapes and Area

Perimeters and Areas

1   This shape has been drawn on a centimetre grid.

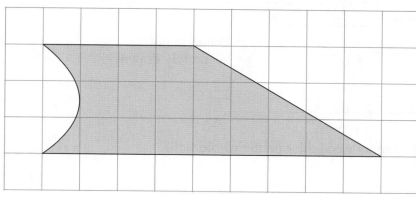

Estimate the area of the shape.
Give the units of your answer.

....

[Total 2 marks]

2   The shape below is drawn on a grid of centimetre squares.

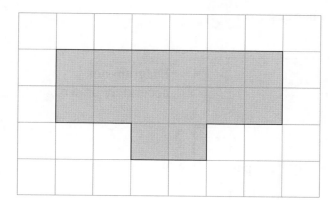

a) What is the perimeter of the shape?

.... cm
[1]

b) What is the area of the shape?

.... cm²
[1]

[Total 2 marks]

3   The diagram below shows a rectangle and a square.

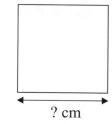

6.4 cm

10 cm

? cm

Diagram not
accurately drawn.

a) Calculate the area of the rectangle.

.... cm²
[2]

b) The rectangle and the square have the same area.
What is the length of each side of the square?

.... cm
[2]

[Total 4 marks]

Section Four — Shapes and Area

4 The diagram shows a field. A farmer wants to spray weedkiller on the field.
Weedkiller costs £0.27 per 10 m^2.

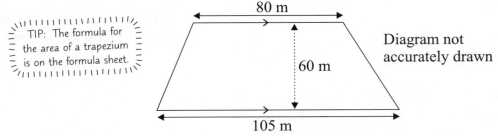

TIP: The formula for the area of a trapezium is on the formula sheet.

80 m

60 m

Diagram not accurately drawn

105 m

How much will it cost the farmer to spray weedkiller on the whole field?

£ ....
[Total 4 marks]

5 Lynn is designing a garden. The diagram shows her design.

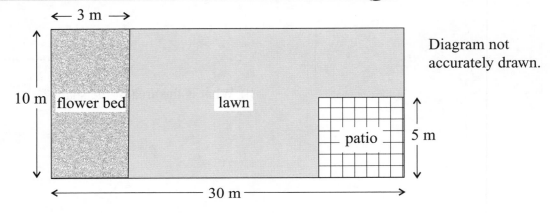

← 3 m →

10 m

flower bed

lawn

patio

5 m

30 m

Diagram not accurately drawn.

Lynn's garden will be rectangular, with a rectangular flower bed at one end, and a square patio at the other end. The rest of the space is taken up by a lawn.

a) The grass seed that Lynn is planning to use comes in boxes that cost £7 each. Each box will cover 10 m^2. How much will it cost Lynn to plant the lawn?

£ ....
[6]

b) Lynn wants to put a decorative border all around the edges of the lawn. Lawn edging is sold in 2 metre strips. How many strips should Lynn buy?

....
[3]

[Total 9 marks]

Score:

21

Section Four — Shapes and Area

Circles

1 The diagram shows a circle with centre O.
A, B and C are points on the circle.

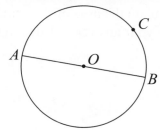

a) What is the term given to the line AB?

....

[1]

b) Draw a straight line from the centre, O, to the edge of the circle.
What is the term given to this line?

....

[1]

c) Draw a line connecting points B and C.
What is the term given to this line?

....

[1]

d) At point A, draw a tangent to the circle.

[1]

[Total 4 marks]

2 The radius of a circle is 0.25 m.

Calculate the circumference of the circle.
Use $\pi = 3.14$ in this calculation.

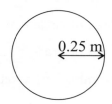

0.25 m

.... m

[Total 2 marks]

3 The diagram shows six identical chocolate biscuits on a rectangular tray.

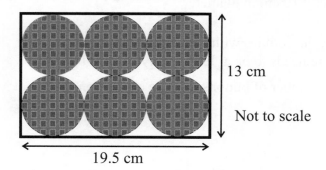

13 cm

Not to scale

19.5 cm

a) Calculate the area of the tray.

.... cm²

[2]

b) Calculate the area of one chocolate biscuit.
Give your answer in cm² to 1 decimal place.

.... cm²

[3]

[Total 5 marks]

Section Four — Shapes and Area

4 A semicircle has a diameter of 18.4 mm.

Calculate the area of the semicircle.
Give your answer to 1 decimal place.

.... mm²

[Total 3 marks]

5 Lucas has a square garden with sides of length 8 metres.
The garden contains a circular paved area.

Lucas wants to sow grass seed on the unpaved parts (shaded below).

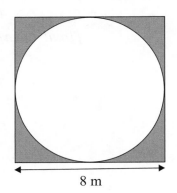

8 m

A packet of grass seeds will sow 0.5 m² of grass.
Calculate the number of packets that Lucas needs to buy.

Area of square = ... × .... = ... m²

Area of circle = π × .... = ... m²

Area of grass = ... − .... = ... m²

Number of packets of grass seed = ... ÷ 0.5 = ...

....

[Total 6 marks]

6 Zara is making cookies for a baking competition.
She makes them exactly 10 cm in diameter.

Zara wants to decorate the cookies with chocolate buttons.
She works out that there needs to be at least 3 cm² for each button.

What is the maximum number of buttons that she can put on each cookie?

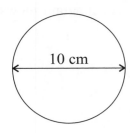

10 cm

....

[Total 5 marks]

Exam Practice Tip

Don't mix up radius and diameter — it seems obvious, but lots of people muddle them up in exams. The radius of a circle is half of its diameter. Think carefully about which one you're being given, and which one you need for a formula. You won't be given the formulas in the exam, so make sure you know them off by heart.

Score

25

Volume

1 The diagram below shows a prism made from centimetre cubes.

Calculate the volume of the prism.

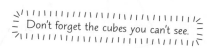
Don't forget the cubes you can't see.

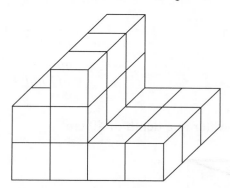

.... cm³

[Total 2 marks]

2 The diagram shows an open-topped cardboard box in the shape of a cuboid.

Calculate the volume of the box.

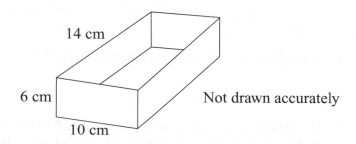

14 cm

6 cm

10 cm

Not drawn accurately

.... cm³

[Total 2 marks]

FUNCTIONAL

3 The diagram below shows Amy's new paddling pool.
It has a diameter of 2 metres, and is 40 cm high.

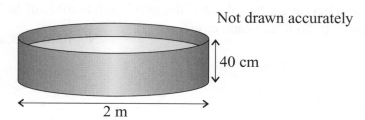

Not drawn accurately

40 cm

2 m

Calculate the volume of water if the paddling pool is completely full.
Give your answer in m³ to 2 decimal places.

Area of cross-section = π × .... = ...

Volume of paddling pool = ... × area of cross-section

= .... × ....

= ....

.... m³

[Total 3 marks]

Section Four — Shapes and Area

4 | Find the volume of the triangular prism shown below.

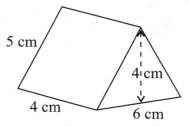

5 cm

4 cm

4 cm

6 cm

Not drawn accurately

.... cm³

[Total 3 marks]

5 | A fish tank of length 90 cm and width 30 cm is filled with water to a depth of 40 cm.

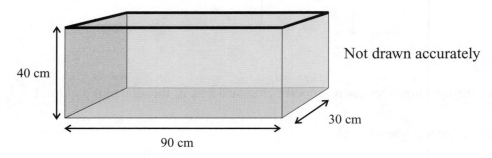

Not drawn accurately

40 cm

30 cm

90 cm

a) Calculate the volume of water in the tank.

.... cm³

[2]

b) To avoid overcrowding in the tank, each fish needs 6000 cm³ of water.
   Work out the greatest number of fish the tank will hold.

....

[2]

[Total 4 marks]

FUNCTIONAL

*6 | A company makes boxes of fudge. Each box is a cube with a side length of 8 cm.

The fudge is packed and sent in packing cases that have length 50 cm,
width 40 cm and height 16 cm. What is the maximum number of fudge
boxes that can be packed into each case?

Not drawn accurately

16 cm

40 cm

50 cm

....

[Total 3 marks]

Score:

17

Section Four — Shapes and Area

Nets

1   Complete the net of the cuboid below.

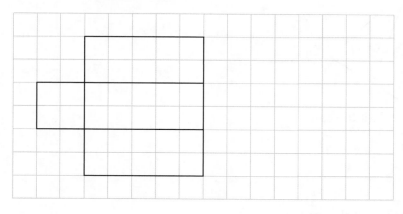

[Total 2 marks]

2   Look at the diagrams below.

A   **B**   **C**   **D**

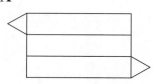   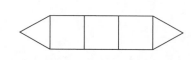   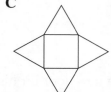   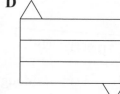

Which diagram shows the net for a triangular prism?

....

[Total 1 mark]

3   Sarah wants to make a box that is 1 cm high, 3 cm wide and 4 cm long, with a closed top.

a) Draw an accurate net of the box.

[3]

b) Calculate the total area of card needed to make the box.
    Assume that no overlap is needed.

.... cm²

[3]

[Total 6 marks]

Section Four — Shapes and Area

4 Here is a square-based pyramid.

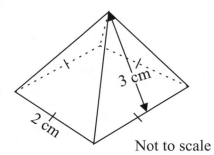

Not to scale

Draw an accurate net of the pyramid on the centimetre grid on the right.

[Total 3 marks]

FUNCTIONAL

5 Dan has bought a new door for his garden shed. He needs to varnish the door all over to make sure that it is weatherproof. The door is 2 m high, 1 m wide, and 3 cm thick.

One tin of varnish will cover 2.45 m² of wood, and Dan will need to give the door two coats of varnish. How many tins should he buy?

Make sure you convert all the measurements into the same units.

....

[Total 4 marks]

6 The diagram shows a regular octahedron and one of its faces. Each of the faces is an equilateral triangle.

Calculate the surface area of the octahedron.

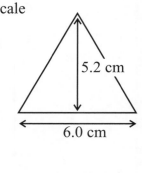

Not to scale

Area of triangle = $\frac{1}{2}$ × .... × ....

= .... cm²

Surface area of octahedron = ... × ....

= .... cm²

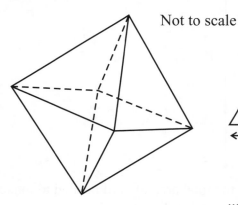

.... cm²

[Total 3 marks]

Score:

19

Section Four — Shapes and Area

Measuring and Drawing Lines and Angles

1 AB is a straight line. **(G)**

A ————————————————————— B

a) Measure the length of AB.

.... cm

[1]

b) Mark the midpoint of the line AB with a cross.

[1]

[Total 2 marks]

2 Triangle ABC is shown below.

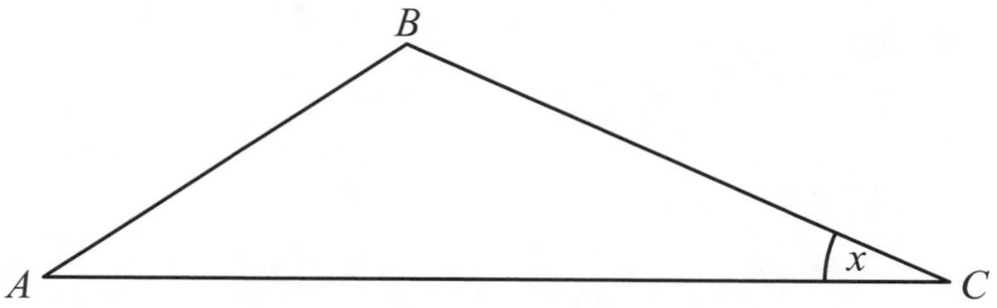

a) Mark with a cross the point on the line AB that is 2.5 cm from A. **(G)**

[1]

b) Measure the length of the line AC. Give your answer in centimetres. **(G)**

.... cm

[1]

c) Measure the angle BAC. **(F)**

.... °

[1]

d) Write down the special name for the type of angle marked x. **(F)**

....

[1]

[Total 4 marks]

3 The diagram shows an angle. **(F)**

What is the special name for this type of angle?

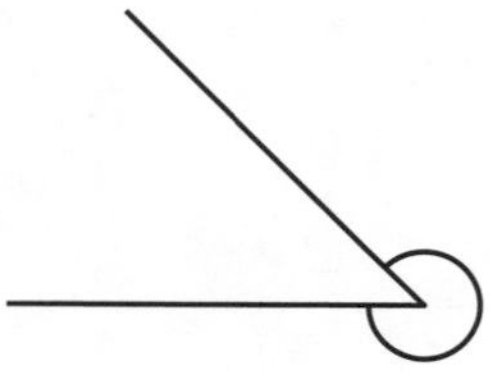

....

[Total 1 mark]

4   The diagram below shows a quadrilateral.

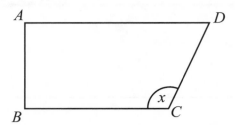

a) Mark a right angle with the letter R.

[1]

b) Measure the length in centimetres of the line *AD*. Ⓖ

.... cm
[1]

c) Write down the special name for the type of angle marked *x*. Ⓕ

....
[1]

d) Measure the size of the angle *x*. Ⓕ

...............................°
[1]

[Total 4 marks]

5   Here is a sketch of triangle *XYZ*. Ⓕ

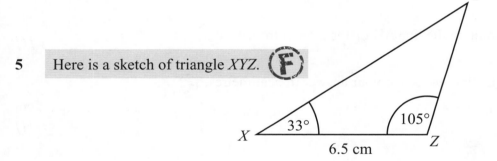

Draw an accurate diagram of triangle *XYZ* in the space below.

[Total 3 marks]

Exam Practice Tip	**Score**

Measuring and drawing lines and angles is all about taking your time and being careful — exciting stuff.
Make sure you've lined the ruler or the protractor up properly and double-check you're reading the right scale.
And finally, if you're measuring in mm or degrees, round to the nearest marking if there isn't one that's bang on.

14

Five Angle Rules

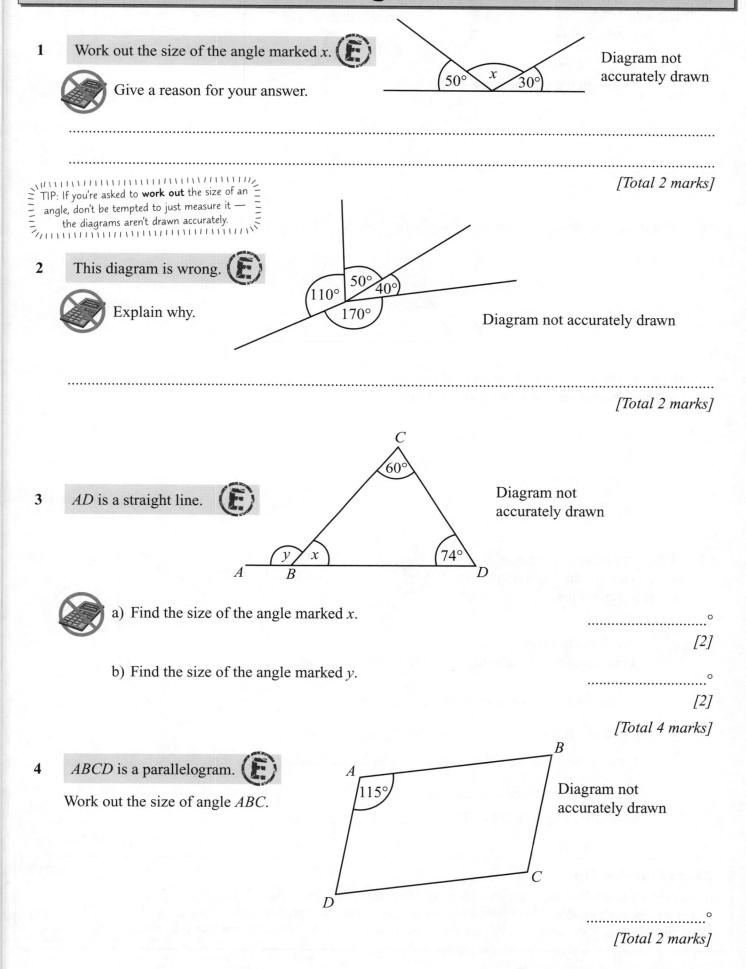

1 Work out the size of the angle marked x.

Give a reason for your answer.

....

....

[Total 2 marks]

TIP: If you're asked to **work out** the size of an angle, don't be tempted to just measure it — the diagrams aren't drawn accurately.

2 This diagram is wrong.

Explain why.

Diagram not accurately drawn

....

[Total 2 marks]

3 AD is a straight line.

Diagram not accurately drawn

a) Find the size of the angle marked x.

......................°

[2]

b) Find the size of the angle marked y.

......................°

[2]

[Total 4 marks]

4 $ABCD$ is a parallelogram.

Work out the size of angle ABC.

Diagram not accurately drawn

......................°

[Total 2 marks]

Section Five — Angles and Geometry

5   *ABC* is an isosceles triangle.
AB = *BC*.
AD is a straight line.

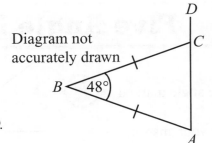

Diagram not
accurately drawn

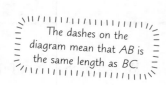

The dashes on the
diagram mean that *AB* is
the same length as *BC*.

   Work out the size of angle *BCD*.

.............................°

[Total 3 marks]

---

*6   *BCDE* is a quadrilateral. Angle *CDE* is a right angle. *AF* is a straight line.

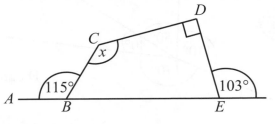

Diagram not
accurately drawn

Work out the size of the angle marked *x*.
Give reasons for each stage of your working.

.............................°

[Total 5 marks]

---

*7   *VXY* is an isosceles triangle. *VX* = *XY*.
UVY is a right-angled triangle.
XZ is a straight line.

Diagram not
accurately drawn

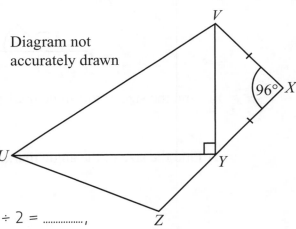

Work out the size of angle *UYZ*.
Give reasons for each stage of your working.

Angles in a triangle add up to ....

.... − 96° = ..., so angle *VYX* = ... ÷ 2 = ...,

because isosceles triangles have ....

Angles on a straight line add up to ....,

so angle *UYZ* = 180° − 90° − .... = ...

.............................°

[Total 4 marks]

Exam Practice Tip

If you can't see how to find the angle you've been asked for, try finding other angles in the diagram first
— chances are you'll be able to use them to find the one you need. You'll probably have to use a few of the
angle rules to get to the answer — if you get stuck just try each rule until you get to one that you can use.

Score

22

Parallel Lines

1 This is an accurately drawn quadrilateral.

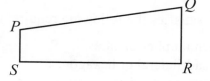

a) Mark with arrows a pair of parallel lines.

[1]

b) Which line is perpendicular to line *QR*?

....

[1]

[Total 2 marks]

2 Find the size of the angle marked *a*.
Give a reason for your answer.

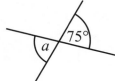

....

[Total 2 marks]

3 *AC* and *DF* are parallel.
GD is a straight line.
CDE is an isosceles triangle.

Find the size of the angle marked *x*.

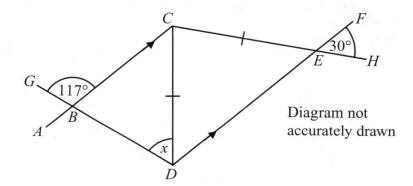

Diagram not
accurately drawn

..............................°

[Total 3 marks]

4 Find the size of the angles marked *a*, *b*, *c* and *d*.

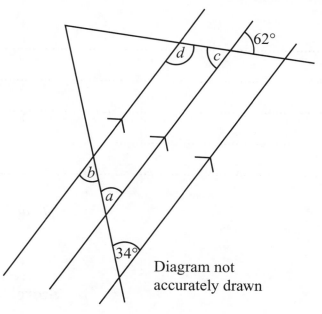

Diagram not
accurately drawn

a = ...°

b = ...°

c = ...°

d = ...°

[Total 4 marks]

Score:

11

Polygons and Angles

1 A polygon satisfies the following requirements: **D**

It has an even number of sides.
It is not a quadrilateral or hexagon.
It has fewer than ten sides.
Five of the interior angles are each equal to 117°.
The remaining interior angles are all equal to each another.

Work out the size of one of the remaining interior angles.

..........................°
[Total 6 marks]

2 The diagram shows a regular pentagon and an equilateral triangle. **D**

Work out the size of the angle *p*.

Diagram not accurately drawn

..........................°
[Total 4 marks]

3 Explain why interior angles in a quadrilateral always add up to 360°. **D**

....
....
....
....
....

[Total 3 marks]

Score:

13

Transformations

1 Reflect the shaded shape in the mirror line.

TIP: Take each corner one by one, reflect it, and then join them all up.

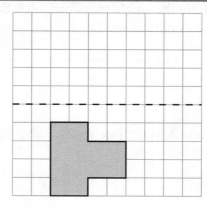

mirror line

[Total 1 mark]

2 Triangle **A** has been drawn on the grid below.

Reflect triangle **A** in the line $x = -1$. Label your image **B**.

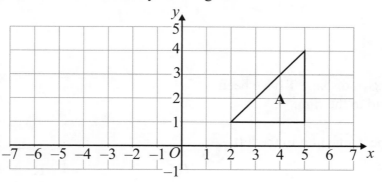

[Total 2 marks]

3 The grid shows triangle **P** and triangle **Q**.

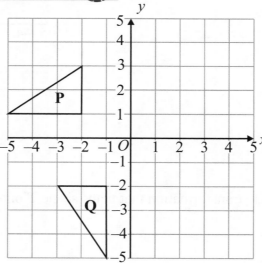

a) Rotate triangle **P** 90° clockwise about the point $(-1, -1)$. *[3]*

b) Describe fully the single transformation that maps triangle **P** onto triangle **Q**.

....

[3]

[Total 6 marks]

Section Five — Angles and Geometry

4 The grid to the right shows shape **A** and shape **B**. (D)

a) Describe fully the single transformation that maps shape **A** onto shape **B**.

....

....

[2]

b) Reflect shape **A** in the line $y = x$. Label the image **C**.

[2]

c) Describe fully the single transformation that maps shape **C** onto shape **B**.

....

[3]

[Total 7 marks]

5 Shape **R**, shape **S** and shape **T** have been drawn on the grid to the right.

a) Translate shape **T** one unit to the left (D) and three units up.

[1]

b) Describe fully the single transformation that maps shape **T** onto shape **R**. (D)

....

[2]

c) Describe fully the single transformation that maps shape **R** onto shape **S**. (C)

....

....

[3]

[Total 6 marks]

Section Five — Angles and Geometry

6 On the grid enlarge the triangle by a scale factor of 3, centre (–4, 0).

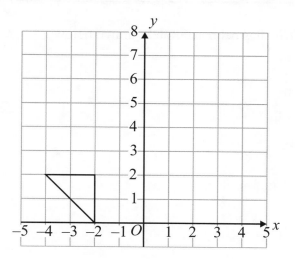

[Total 3 marks]

7 Shape **A** has been drawn on the grid.

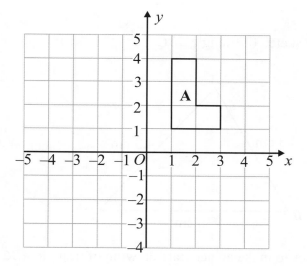

Shape **A** is reflected in the *x*-axis to give shape **B**.
Shape **B** is rotated 180° about the origin to give shape **C**.

Describe fully the single transformation which maps shape **A** onto shape **C**.

....

[Total 4 marks]

Exam Practice Tip

Make sure you give all the details when you describe a transformation — if a question is worth three marks then you'll probably need to give three bits of information. For example, for enlargements give the scale factor and the centre of enlargement, and for rotations give the centre, the direction and the angle of rotation.

Score

29

Section Five — Angles and Geometry

Triangle Construction

1   Side *BC* of the equilateral triangle *ABC* has been accurately drawn below.

B ———————————————— C

a) Use a ruler and compasses to complete the accurate drawing of triangle *ABC*.   *[1]*

b) Construct the bisector of angle *ACB* of the triangle. Ⓒ   *[2]*
   You must show all your construction lines.

[Total 3 marks]

2   The diagram below is a sketch of triangle *ABC*. Ⓔ

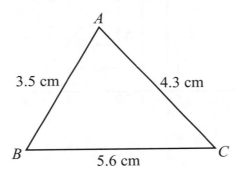

Diagram not
accurately drawn

Use a ruler and compasses to make an accurate drawing of triangle *ABC* in the space below.
You must show all your construction lines.

[Total 3 marks]

Score:

6

Section Five — Angles and Geometry

Loci and Constructions

1 Use a ruler and compasses to construct the perpendicular bisector of the line below.

[Total 2 marks]

2 Use a ruler and compasses to construct the bisector of the angle below.

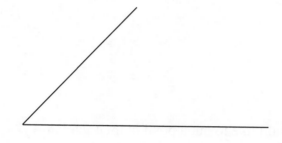

[Total 2 marks]

3 Salman has a robot which can walk a maximum of 10 m from the beam AB.

Shade the region on the diagram where Salman's robot can walk, using the scale shown.

A ——————————————————— B

Scale: 1 cm represents 5 m

[Total 2 marks]

4 Shade the region that is both nearer to P than Q, and that is less than 4.3 cm from Q.

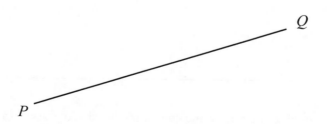

[Total 3 marks]

Section Five — Angles and Geometry

5 A town council wants to put up a new visitor information board. They think that it should be placed closer to the park than to the library, but also closer to the station than to the park.

The diagram below shows a scale map of the town centre.
Shade in the region of the town where the board could be placed.

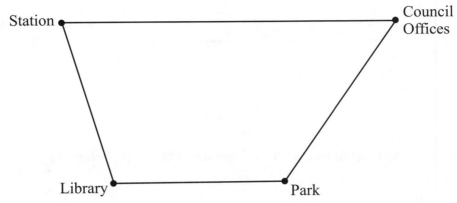

[Total 5 marks]

6 Hilary and Tony are deciding where they would like to put a pond in their garden.
Hilary wants the centre of the pond to be 1 m from the garden wall *BC*.
Tony wants the centre of the pond to be 2 m from the tree *F*.

Accurately complete the plan of the garden below by using a cross (✕) to mark any points where Hilary and Tony would both be happy for the centre of the pond to be.

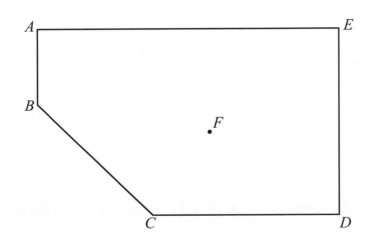

Scale: 1 cm represents 1 m

[Total 4 marks]

Exam Practice Tip

You won't always be told that you need to use a ruler and compasses, but if you're asked to <u>construct</u> something then you'll be expected to use them. Make sure you don't rub out your construction lines — even if it doesn't ask for them in the question you won't get all the marks unless you show how you did your construction.

Score

18

Pythagoras' Theorem

1 Below is a right-angled triangle.

Find the length of the side marked x.
Give your answer to an appropriate degree of accuracy.

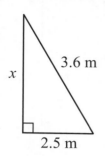

.... m

[Total 3 marks]

FUNCTIONAL

*2 Alison and Rob want to put a water pipe across their rectangular field.
The diagram below shows their field.

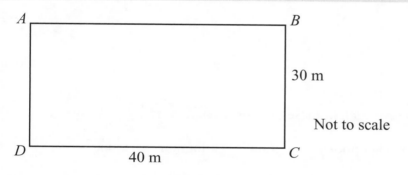

30 m

Not to scale

40 m

> TIP: Draw a quick sketch using the information that you're given in the question — then you can easily see where to put the numbers in the Pythagoras formula.

The pipe must run from a tap at point at A to the shed at point C.

Alison wants to put the pipe across the diagonal of the field.
Rob wants to put the pipe round the edge of the field.

The pipe costs £8.35 per metre.

If they put the pipe across the diagonal they will have to dig a trench and replace the grass,
which will cost £202.50. If they put the pipe round the edge they will not have to dig a trench.

Which option is cheaper? Explain your answer.

....

....

[Total 6 marks]

Exam Practice Tip

You probably won't be <u>told</u> to use Pythagoras' theorem in the question — you'll have to remember it's something you can use if you've got two sides of a right-angled triangle and you're looking for the third side.
If you get a wordy question it's a good idea to sketch a diagram to make sure your sides are in the right place.

Score

9

Converting Units

1   The table below shows different units of measurements.

a) Complete the table using the most appropriate unit of measurement.

	Imperial	**Metric**
Length of a skirt	inches	....
Weight of a rabbit	....	kilograms
Volume of a milk jug	pints	....

[3]

b) The length of a classroom is 887 cm. How long is that in metres?

.... m

[1]

c) A bunch of bananas weighs 1.3 kg. How much is this in grams?

.... g

[1]

[Total 5 marks]

2   How accurately should you give each of these measurements?

Choose from one of the following options: gram   kilogram   tonne

a) The weight of a pencil.

to the nearest ....

[1]

b) The weight of an aircraft carrier.

to the nearest ....

[1]

[Total 2 marks]

FUNCTIONAL

3   Emma is having a party with some friends.

   She has 2.5 litres of orange juice.
How many 250 ml cups can be filled from it?

.... cups

[Total 3 marks]

4 The formula to convert kilometres (k) to miles (m) is $m = \dfrac{5k}{8}$.

a) How many miles is 40 km? (E)

.... miles
[2]

b) A giraffe can run at 60 km/h.
Show that a giraffe could be outrun by a camel running at 40 mph. (D)

....

....

[2]

[Total 4 marks]

FUNCTIONAL

5 Nicole wants to post some books to a friend in another country.
Each book weighs 1.5 lb and each package can hold a maximum weight of 2500 g. (E)

How many books can she send in one package?

Hint — you need to do a conversion between kilograms and pounds.

....

[Total 4 marks]

FUNCTIONAL

6 1 litre = $1\frac{3}{4}$ pints. (C)

Margaret needs 14 pints of water to fill up her fish tank.
She uses three different sized containers to fill up the tank.
One container holds 520 ml, one holds 540 ml and the other holds 720 ml.

You could start by converting 14 pints into litres.

To fill up the tank, Margaret uses the 720 ml container three times,
the 520 ml container five times and then the 540 ml container to finish filling it up.

How many times must she fill up the 540 ml container to finish filling the fish tank?

....

[Total 5 marks]

Exam Practice Tip

Make sure you learn the rough conversions between metric units (kg, km and litres) and imperial units (pounds, miles and pints). I know it's dull just memorising numbers, but you might not be given them in the exam. You also need to know metric-to-metric conversions, but thankfully those are MUCH easier.

Score

23

Reading Scales

1 Give the readings from each of the scales below.

a)
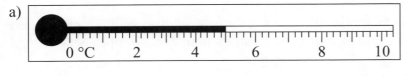

.... °C
[1]

b)
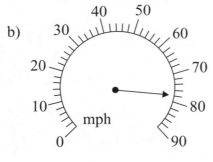

.... mph
[1]

c)
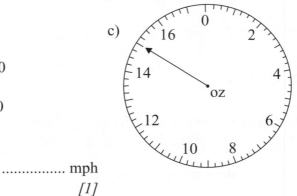

.... oz
[1]

[Total 3 marks]

2 Francis has a bottle of ink, as shown below.

a) How much ink does he have left in the bottle?

.... ml
[1]

b) Francis uses 15 ml of the ink.
How much does he now have left?

.... ml
[2]

[Total 3 marks]

3 Alex is competing in a javelin competition.

a) Her best throw of the day is shown below. How far did she throw?

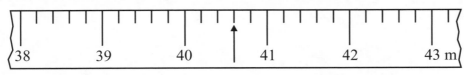

.... m
[1]

b) Martin threw the javelin 42.4 m. Mark his throw on the tape measure above.

[1]

[Total 2 marks]

Score:

8

Section Six — Measures

Rounding and Estimating Measurements

1 The man in this picture is of average height.

Use this information to estimate the height of the penguin.

.... cm

[Total 3 marks]

2 Mandy uses a thermometer to measure the temperature outside.

a) The thermometer on the left shows the temperature first thing in the morning.
   Write down the temperature. (F)

.... °C
[1]

b) By the afternoon the temperature is 1.2 °C.
   Mark the temperature on the thermometer to the right.
[1]

c) The next morning, Mandy records the temperature as 3 °C to the nearest degree.
   What is the minimum temperature her thermometer could show in order for her to record this temperature?

.... °C
[1]

[Total 3 marks]

3 Joseph is weighing himself. His scales give his weight to the nearest kilogram. (C)

According to his scales, Joseph is 57 kg.
What are the upper and lower bounds of his weight?

Upper bound: .... kg

Lower bound: .... kg
[Total 2 marks]

Score:

8

Reading Timetables

1 Amir flies from London to Chicago, setting off in the morning. **(F)**

a) The clock shows the time when the flight leaves.
What time is shown on the clock?

....
[1]

b) The time in Chicago is 5 hours behind the time in London.
What time is it in Chicago when it is 10:30 am in London.?

....
[1]

[Total 2 marks]

2 Deirdre is planning a train journey. **(F)**

a) It will take 25 minutes to get to the station and she wants to be there at 11:15.
What is the latest time she should leave home?

....
[2]

b) The train leaves at 11:35 and arrives at 13:22.
How long is the journey? Give your answer in minutes.

.... minutes
[2]

[Total 4 marks]

FUNCTIONAL

3 Part of the bus timetable from Coventry to Rugby is shown below.

Coventry	14:45	16:15	17:45
Bubbenhall	–	16:40	18:10
Stretton	15:14	16:54	18:24
Birdingbury	–	17:04	–
Rugby	15:35	17:30	18:40

The dashes on the timetable mean the bus doesn't stop.

a) What time does the 16:15 bus from Coventry leave Birdingbury? **(F)**

....
[1]

b) Lisa arrives at Birdingbury bus stop at 16:58. **(F)**
How long will she have to wait for the bus to Rugby?

.... minutes
[1]

The 16:15 bus from Coventry continues to Lutterworth after Rugby. It arrives in Lutterworth at 18:15.

c) Anne lives in Bubbenhall. If she catches this bus from her home, **(E)**
how long will it take her to get to Lutterworth?

.... h .... mins
[2]

[Total 4 marks]

Section Six — Measures

4 The timetable shows the shifts that five waitresses worked one night at a restaurant. **(F)**

a) Who worked the longest shift?

....

[1]

b) How long was Avril's shift?

....

[1]

c) Write down the times that there were at least four waitresses working.

....

....

[2]

[Total 4 marks]

FUNCTIONAL

5 Phileas has arrived in San Francisco on holiday.
There is a world clock at the airport in San Francisco. **(E)**

08:36 Wednesday	16:36 Wednesday	05:36 Wednesday
San Francisco	Paris	Hawaii

He needs to call a friend in Paris at 07:15 on Thursday, Paris time.
What time and day is this in San Francisco?

Time: .... Day: ....

[Total 3 marks]

Score: ☐

17

Bearings and Maps

1 The diagram shows the positions of two points on a map.

X is the top of a mountain. Y is the location of a group of hikers.

a) A hiker is injured, and the rescue team need to know the location of the hikers.
Measure and write down the bearing of Y from X.

.... °
[1]

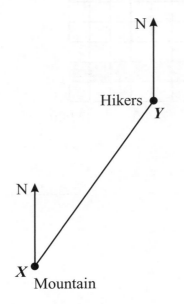

b) There is another group of hikers at a bearing of 100° from Y.
Draw a line on the diagram to show the direction of the second group.

[1]

[Total 2 marks]

2 This map is drawn to a scale of 1 : 200 000.

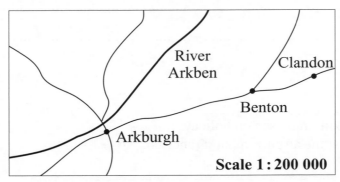

a) Work out the actual distance, in km, between Arkburgh and Benton.

.... km
[1]

b) Madeline cycles 7 km to school. How far would this be on the map?

.... cm
[1]

[Total 2 marks]

Score:

4

Section Six — Measures

Speed

1   John and Alan hired a van. Their receipt gave them information about how much time they spent travelling in the van, and how fast they went.

> Travelling time: 1 hour 15 minutes
> Average Speed: 56 km/h

Calculate the distance that John and Alan travelled in the van.

.... km

[Total 2 marks]

2   Beatrix is on a cycling holiday in Cumbria.
The table below shows the distances between each of the places she visits.

Keswick		
26 miles	**Windermere**	
33 miles	5 miles	**Hawkshead**

On Friday it took her 45 minutes to cycle from Hawkshead to Windermere.

On Saturday, she then cycled from Windermere, arriving in Keswick $3\frac{1}{4}$ hours later.

On Sunday, she cycled back from Keswick to Hawkshead in 3 hours 45 minutes.

*a) On which day did Beatrix ride her bike at the fastest average speed?

....

[4]

b) Work out Beatrix's average cycling speed over all three days. Give your answer to 1 decimal place.

Overall speed = $\dfrac{\text{........................}}{\text{..................}}$

$= \dfrac{\text{..........} + \text{..........} + \text{..........}}{\text{..........} + \text{..........} + \text{..........}} = \dfrac{\text{..............}}{\text{..............}} = \text{..............}$ mph

.... mph

[3]

[Total 7 marks]

Score:

9

Section Six — Measures

Collecting Data

1   Faye wants to find out how often teenagers buy chocolate bars. **C**

She writes the following question to ask in a survey.

> How many chocolate bars have you bought?
>
> 1 – 2   2 – 3   3 – 4

Write two things that are wrong with the question above.

1. ....

2. ....

[Total 2 marks]

2   Mike wants to find out how often people in his year group go to watch football matches. **C**

He includes the question below in a survey.

> How often do you go to watch football matches?
>
> Sometimes   A lot

a) Give **one** thing that is wrong with this question.

....

....

[1]

Mike decides to ask the boys in his football team to do his survey.

b) Give one reason why this sample may not give him reliable information.

....

....

[1]

[Total 2 marks]

Exam Practice Tip

In the exam, you might be asked to say why a particular survey question isn't very good. Always look at two things — the way it's worded and whether the response boxes are suitable. You might also get asked why a particular sample isn't good. Bias is often the problem here — think about whether the sample is representative.

Score

4

Mean, Median, Mode and Range

1 One evening Preya makes 10 phone calls. When the bill comes it shows **F** how long each call was, in minutes. The call lengths are listed below.

   10   12   25   3   37   13   12   18   41   33

a) Work out the median length of Preya's calls.

.... minutes

[2]

b) Calculate the mean phone call length.
   Give your answer to the nearest minute.

.... minutes

[2]

c) What is the range?

.... minutes

[2]

[Total 6 marks]

2 Company A employs 5 people.
   Their annual salaries are listed below.

   £18 000   £38 500   £18 000   £25 200   £18 000

a) Write down the mode. **F**

£ ....

[1]

b) What is the median annual salary? **F**

£ ....

[1]

Company B has a mean annual salary of £24 150.

c) Compare the mean annual salary of Company A and Company B. **E**

....

....

[3]

[Total 5 marks]

3 Sam thinks of three different whole numbers. **F**

   The numbers have a range of 6 and a mean of 4.
   What are the three numbers?

.................., ..., ...

[Total 2 marks]

Exam Practice Tip

Remember — the mode is the most common value, the median is the middle value (when the data is written in order), the mean is the sum of all the values divided by the number of values, and the range is the highest value minus the lowest value. It's usually a good idea to write your data in ascending order before you do anything else.

Score

13

Tables

1   Ryan is looking at properties in a new development.
    The table below shows information on these properties.

Property name	House/apartment	No. of bedrooms	Size (square feet)	Price (£)
The Apricot	House	5	1136	319 995
The Ivy	Apartment	2	526	119 995
The Lavender	House	3	744	189 995
The Oak	House	4	892	244 995
The Willow	Apartment	3	608	144 995

a) Which property has the fewest bedrooms?

....

[1]

b) How many of these properties are **houses** that are smaller than 1000 square feet?

....

[1]

[Total 2 marks]

FUNCTIONAL

*2 Mr and Mrs White and their three children want to go on holiday next year.
    They can go for a week in either June or July.
    The table below shows prices in £ per adult and per child for a week.

Departure Date	Adult	Child
01 Jan — 19 Mar	140	125
20 Mar — 21 May	180	150
22 May — 30 Jun	300	290
01 July — 8 Sep	330	275
9 Sep — 26 Nov	230	160
27 Nov — 31 Dec	270	210

Compare the cost of the White family going on holiday for a week in June with the cost
of a week in July.

....

....

....

....

....

[Total 4 marks]

Score:

6

Pictograms

1 This pictogram shows the number of jars of jam sold in a campsite shop in one month. (G)

a) How many jars of strawberry jam were sold?

....
[1]

Strawberry Jam	🍓🍓🍓🍓
Blackberry Jam	🍓🍓◗
Raspberry Jam	

🍓 Represents 10 jars

The shop sold 35 jars of raspberry jam.
b) Complete the pictogram. *[1]*

c) Which jam did they sell the least of?

....
[1]

[Total 3 marks]

2 This pictogram shows the number of eggs laid by some chickens (G) at a farm on Monday, Tuesday and Wednesday.

Monday	○ ○ ○ ◖
Tuesday	○ ○ ◖
Wednesday	○ ○ ○ ○ ○
Thursday	
Friday	

○ = 8 eggs

Pay attention to the key, which shows how many things each symbol stands for.

a) How many eggs were laid on Monday?

....
[1]

b) How many more eggs were laid on Wednesday than Tuesday?

....
[1]

24 eggs were laid on Thursday.
18 eggs were laid on Friday.

c) Show this information on the pictogram. *[2]*

[Total 4 marks]

Score: ⬜

7

 ⬜   ⬜   ⬜

Section Seven — Statistics and Probability

Bar Charts

1 The dual bar chart below shows the number of cups of tea and coffee sold in a cafe each day.

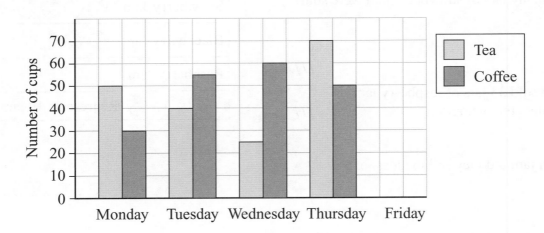

a) How many cups of tea were sold on Wednesday?

....

[1]

b) On which day did the cafe sell 15 more cups of coffee than tea?

....

[1]

On Friday, the cafe sold 45 cups of tea and 30 cups of coffee.
c) Show this information on the bar chart.

[2]

d) Over the 5 days, did the cafe sell more cups of tea or coffee?

....

[2]

[Total 6 marks]

2 This table shows some information about the favourite sports of some students.

Sport	Students
Football	14
Swimming	5
Athletics	9
Netball	1
Hockey	6

Show this information as a bar chart on the grid below.

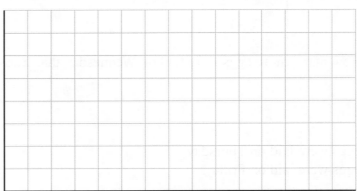

[Total 3 marks]

Score:

9

Pie Charts

1   A survey was carried out at a leisure centre to find out which sport people prefer to do. The results are shown in the pie chart.

a) What fraction of people prefer to do fitness training?

....
[1]

60 people said they prefer to play football.

b) How many people prefer to play badminton?

....
[2]

[Total 3 marks]

2   A survey was carried out in a local cinema to find out which flavour of popcorn people bought. The results are in the table below.

a) Draw a pie chart to represent the information.

Type of popcorn	Number sold
Plain	12
Salted	18
Sugared	9
Toffee	21

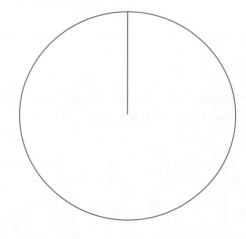

[3]

Another survey was carried out to find out which flavour of ice cream people bought. The results are shown in the pie chart below.

Chris compares the two pie charts and says,

     "The results show that more people chose strawberry ice cream than toffee popcorn."

b) Explain whether or not Chris is right.

....

....

....

....

[1]

[Total 4 marks]

Scatter Graphs

1   The end of year exam results of 15 pupils who study both Spanish and Italian are shown on the scatter graph below.

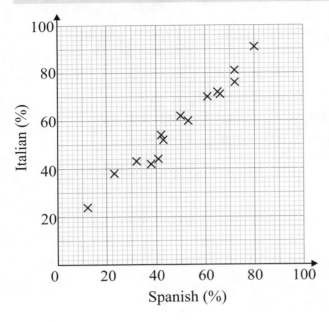

a) What did the pupil who scored 50% on their Spanish exam score in their Italian exam?

.... %

[1]

b) Draw a line of best fit for the data.

[1]

c) Ahmed was absent for his Spanish exam but scored 66% on his Italian exam. Estimate the mark he might have got in Spanish.

.... %

[2]

d) Julia has a hypothesis. She says: "Pupils who score better on their Spanish exam usually also score better on their Italian exam." Comment on this hypothesis.

....

[1]

[Total 5 marks]

2   The heights and weights of boys playing in a rugby team are shown in the scatter graph below.

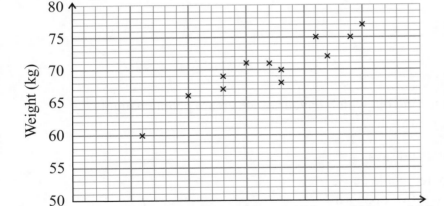

Two more boys join the team. Their heights and weights are shown in the table below.

Player	Height (cm)	Weight (kg)
13	169	70
14	183	76

a) Show this information on the scatter graph.   [1]

b) Describe the type of correlation between the height and weight of the players.

....

[1]

Another player joins the team. He is 176 cm tall.

c) Estimate how much he will weigh.

.... kg

[2]

[Total 4 marks]

Score:

9

Section Seven — Statistics and Probability

Frequency Tables and Averages

1 Tom is having a party and wants to know whether to serve cola, orange juice, lemonade or something else. He conducts a small survey to help him decide. He asks the question: "Which is your favourite drink — cola, orange juice, lemonade or a different drink?" **(F)**

The replies are:

Orange juice	Cola	Other	Cola	Cola
Lemonade	Cola	Orange juice	Other	Orange juice
Orange juice	Cola	Lemonade	Other	Cola
Other	Cola	Other	Lemonade	Orange juice

Drink	Tally	Frequency
Cola		
Orange juice		
Lemonade		
Other		

a) Use the data to complete the table.

[2]

b) Which is the modal drink?

Remember — 'mode is most'.

....

[1]

[Total 3 marks]

2 A traffic survey at a road junction recorded the following numbers of vehicles arriving per minute. **(D)**

Vehicles per minute	0	1	2	3	4
Frequency	13	8	6	2	1

a) What is the median number of vehicles per minute?

....

[2]

b) What is the mean number of vehicles per minute?

....

[3]

[Total 5 marks]

Score:

8

Section Seven — Statistics and Probability

94

Grouped Frequency Tables — Averages

1 As part of their coursework, the students in a Year 11 maths class recorded their arm spans. The results are shown below.

Use the mid-interval value of each arm span group to find an estimate of the mean arm span.

Arm Span, x cm	Frequency	Mid-Interval Value	Frequency × Mid-Interval Value
$120 \le x < 130$	13	$(120 + 130) \div 2 = 125$	$13 \times 125 = ...$
$130 \le x < 140$	6	$(130 + 140) \div 2 = ...$	$6 \times .... = ...$
$140 \le x < 150$	4		
$150 \le x < 160$	7		
Total			

Mean arm span = ... ÷ .... = ...

.... cm

[Total 4 marks]

2 A class of children was asked to draw a 10 cm line without a ruler, and then measure their attempt. This is a table of their results.

Length of line, x cm	Frequency
$8.5 \le x < 9$	3
$9 \le x < 9.5$	2
$9.5 \le x < 10$	12
$10 \le x < 10.5$	8
$10.5 \le x < 11$	5

a) Which group contains the median?

....

[2]

b) What is the modal class?

....

[1]

c) Calculate an estimate of the mean length of their lines.

Hint: you should add some extra columns to the table above to help you.

.... cm

[4]

[Total 7 marks]

Score:

11

Section Seven — Statistics and Probability

Frequency Polygons

1 The grouped frequency table below shows the number of hours of homework 30 students did in one week.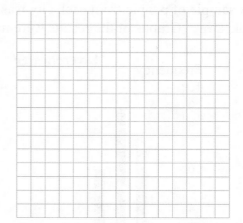

Hours of Homework, x	Frequency
$0 \leq x < 2$	15
$2 \leq x < 4$	7
$4 \leq x < 6$	5
$6 \leq x < 8$	3

Draw a frequency polygon for the data using the grid on the right.

[Total 2 marks]

2 The frequency polygons below show the amount of rainfall per day in two different towns over a period of 45 days.

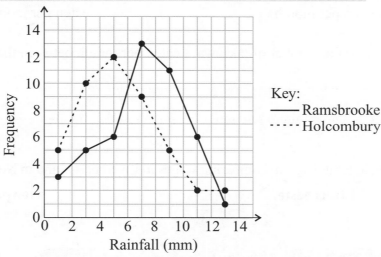

a) Write down one comparison of the amount of rainfall in the two towns.

....

[1]

b) Use the frequency polygon to calculate an estimate of the mean amount of rainfall in Ramsbrooke over the 45 days.

.... mm

[3]

[Total 4 marks]

Score:

6

Section Seven — Statistics and Probability

More Charts and Graphs

1 A newspaper contains an article comparing two different cities, Liverchester and Newpool.

a) A sample of people from each city was asked how many times a month they eat a takeaway. Graphs of the results were included in the article as shown below.

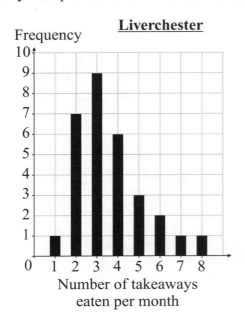

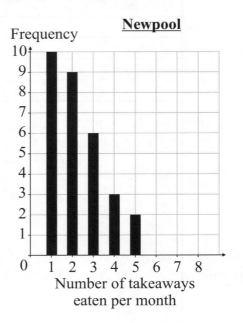

Compare the range of the number of takeaways eaten per month between the two cities.

....

....

[2]

b) The article also includes a diagram comparing wages in Liverchester and in Newpool.

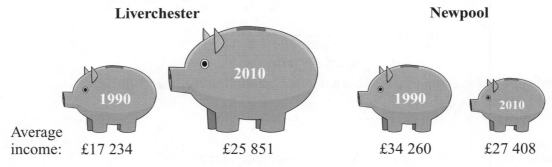

In what way could this information be misunderstood? Give a reason for your answer.

....

....

[2]

[Total 4 marks]

Score: ☐

4

Section Seven — Statistics and Probability

Probability Basics

1 Eva has some picture cards. (F)

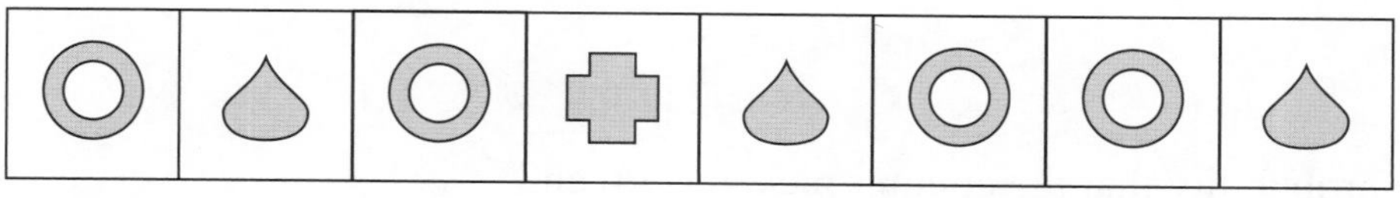

She picks one card without looking.
Choose one of the words below to complete the sentences.

impossible   unlikely   evens   likely   certain

a) It is .... that she chooses ✚. *[1]*

b) It is .... that she chooses ⭕. *[1]*

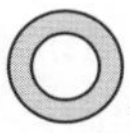

c) It is .... that she chooses ⚡. *[1]*

[Total 3 marks]

2 Ellie rolls a fair 6-sided dice. (F)

a) On the scale below, mark with an arrow (↑) the probability that she will roll an odd number.

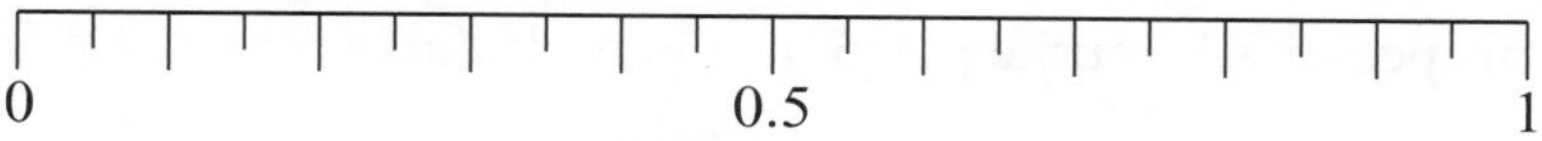

0   0.5   1

[1]

b) On the scale below, mark with an arrow (↑) the probability that she will roll a 0.

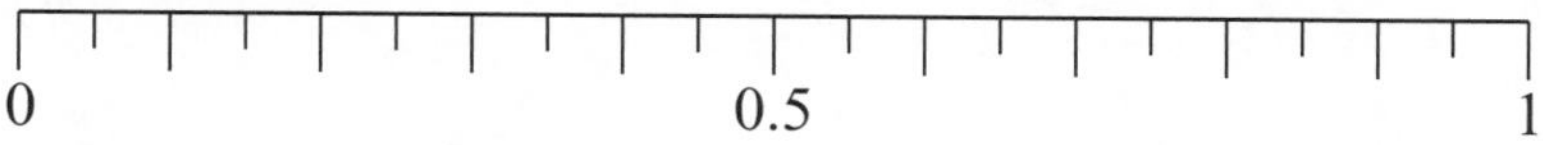

0   0.5   1

[1]

c) What is the probability that Ellie rolls a number larger than 4?
Give your answer as a fraction in its simplest form.

....
[2]

[Total 4 marks]

3 Alecia has an 8-sided spinner labelled as shown on the right. (E)
It has an equal probability of landing on each of the 8 segments.

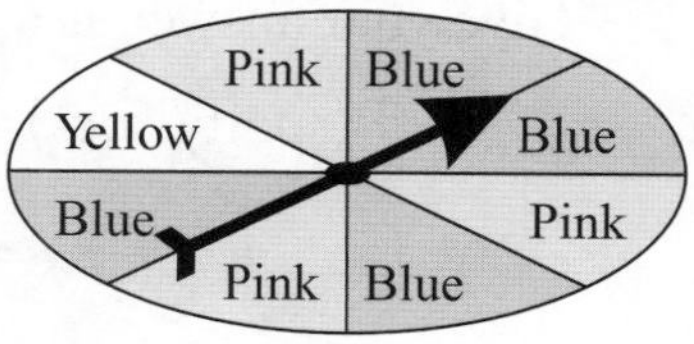

a) What colour segment is the spinner most likely to land on?

....
[1]

b) What is the probability of the spinner landing on a pink segment?

....
[1]

[Total 2 marks]

4 There are 10 counters in a bag. Four of the counters are blue and the rest are red.

One counter is picked out at random.
a) Work out the probability that the counter picked is red.
   Give your answer as a fraction in its simplest form.

....
[2]

b) What is the probability that the counter picked is green?

....
[1]

[Total 3 marks]

5 Steven asks all the members of his football team whether their favourite position is in attack, midfield, defence or goal.
The table below shows his results.

Position	Frequency
Attack	6
Midfield	9
Defence	4
Goal	1

A member of the team is chosen at random.

What is the probability that this person's favourite position is in midfield?

....
[Total 2 marks]

6 Sarah has stripy, spotty and plain socks in her drawer.
She picks out a sock from the drawer at random.

The probability that she will pick a plain sock is 0.4.
The probability that she will pick a spotty sock from the drawer is x.
The probability that she will pick a stripy sock from the drawer is $2x$.

What is the probability that the sock she picks is stripy?
Give your answer as a decimal.

P(spotty sock) = x, P(stripy sock) = 2x, P(plain sock) = 0.4

.... + x + 2x = 1

.... = 1 − .... = ...

x = ... ÷ .... = ...

P(stripy sock) = 2x, so P(stripy sock) = 2 × .... = ...

....
[Total 3 marks]

Score:

17

More Probability

1 Alvar has a fair 6-sided dice and a set of five cards numbered 2, 4, 6, 8 and 10.
He rolls the dice and chooses a card at random.
Alvar adds the number on the dice to the number on the card to calculate his total score.

a) Complete the table below to show all of the possible scores.

Cards

		2	4	6	8	10
Dice	1					
	2					12
	3				11	13
	4			10	12	14
	5		9	11	13	15
	6	8	10	12	14	16

[2]

b) Find the probability that Alvar will score exactly 9.
Give your answer as a fraction in its simplest form.

....
[2]

[Total 4 marks]

2 Lewis has a bag of sweets. There are five different flavours of sweet.
Lewis takes one sweet from the bag at random. The probabilities of
him picking the different flavours are shown below.

Flavour of sweet	Cherry	Mango	Strawberry	Blackcurrant	Lime
Probability	0.16	0.23	0.22	0.28	0.11

Find the probability that Lewis chooses a mango or a blackcurrant flavoured sweet.

....
[Total 2 marks]

Score:

6

Expected Frequency

1 The probability of a train arriving in Udderston on time is 0.64.

Hester gets the train to Udderston 200 times a year.
How many times a year can Hester expect to arrive at the station on time?

.... × 0.64 = ...

....
[Total 2 marks]

2 Here is a 5-sided spinner.
The spinner is biased.

The probability that the spinner will land on the numbers 1 to 4 is given in this table.
I spin the spinner 100 times.

Number	1	2	3	4	5
Probability	0.3	0.15	0.2	0.25	

Estimate the number of times it will land on 5.

....
[Total 4 marks]

3 I play an online game with two levels — easy and hard.

If I win a game on the easy level, I gain 3 points.
If I win a game on the hard level, I gain 8 points.
If I lose a game on either level, I lose 2 points.

The probability of me winning an easy game is $\frac{1}{2}$.

The probability of me winning a hard game is $\frac{1}{5}$.

How many more points should I expect to end up with if I play 20 easy games instead of 20 hard games?

Number of easy games I should expect to win: $20 \times \frac{1}{2}$ = ...,
so I should expect to: gain .... × 3 = ... points
and lose (20 − ....) × .... = ... × .... = ... points.
So overall, I should expect to end up with .... − .... = ... points.

Number of hard games I should expect to win: $20 \times \frac{\text{.......}}{\text{.......}}$ = ...,
so I should expect to: gain .... × 8 = ... points
and lose (......... − ....) × .... = ... × .... = ... points.
So overall, I should expect to end up with .... − .... = ... points.

So I should expect to end up with .... more points playing 20 easy games
than playing 20 hard games.

....
[Total 5 marks]

Score:

11

Section Seven — Statistics and Probability

Relative Frequency

1 A company makes chocolate bars which have biscuit in the middle.

The company wanted to find the probability that one of their chocolate bars has no biscuit in the middle.

They carried out an experiment by picking chocolate bars at random from the production line.

The relative frequency of a chocolate bar without biscuit was recorded after picking 1000 bars, 2000 bars, 3000 bars and 4000 bars.

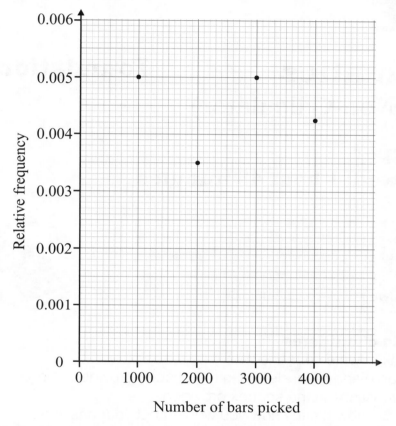

a) Use the graph to find how many of the first 2000 chocolate bars picked had biscuit in the middle.

....

[2]

b) Which of the relative frequencies shown on the graph is the best estimate for the probability a chocolate bar will have no biscuit in the middle? Explain your answer.

....

....

....

[2]

[Total 4 marks]

Exam Practice Tip

Try not to confuse expected and relative frequency.
Expected frequency is the number of times you expect something to happen when you know its probability.
Relative frequency is an estimate of the probability using results from an experiment.

Score

4

Candidate Surname		Candidate Forename(s)	

Centre Number	Candidate Number	Candidate Signature

GCSE

Mathematics

Foundation Tier

Paper 1 (Non-Calculator)

Practice Paper
Time allowed: 1 hour 45 minutes

You must have:
Pen, pencil, eraser, ruler, protractor, pair of compasses.
You may use tracing paper.

You are not allowed to use a calculator.

Instructions to candidates

- Use **black** ink to write your answers.
- Write your name and other details in the spaces provided above.
- Answer **all** questions in the spaces provided.
- In calculations show clearly how you worked out your answers.
- Do all rough work on the paper.

Information for candidates

- The marks available are given in brackets at the end of each question.
- You may get marks for method, even if your answer is incorrect.
- There are 26 questions in this paper. There are no blank pages.
- There are 100 marks available for this paper.
- You will be assessed on the quality of your written communication
  in some questions. These will be clearly marked — take particular
  care here with spelling, punctuation and the quality of explanations.

Get the answers — on video and in print

Your free Online Edition of this book includes a link to step-by-step video solutions
for this Exam Paper, plus worked solutions you can print out.
There's more info about how to get your Online Edition at the front of this book.

Answer ALL the questions.

Write your answers in the spaces provided.

You must show all of your working.

1 (a) What is the value of the 7 in the number 13 973?

....
[1]

(b) Round the number 331 to the nearest 10

....
[1]

(c) Write out the number 1758 in words.

....
[1]

(d) Write 85.7 to the nearest whole number.

....
[1]

2 Draw an accurate net of the cuboid shown on the right. The first face has been drawn for you below.

Diagram not accurately drawn

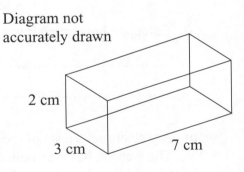

2 cm

3 cm   7 cm

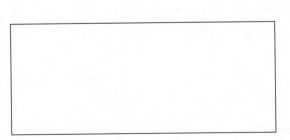

[4]

1

3 (a) Work out 7.55×10

....

[1]

(b) Work out $427.3 \div 100$

....

[1]

(c) Work out 0.302×1000

....

[1]

4 Sam needs to buy grammar books and dictionaries for a class of students.
She needs 15 copies of each. She sees them on sale at a local book shop.

Grammar Book £3   Dictionary £2

(a) Calculate how much it would cost Sam to buy all the books for her class from the shop.

....

....

[2]

(b) A website sells a set of the same grammar book and dictionary together for £4.
The website has a £5 delivery charge.
Should Sam buy the books from the shop or the website? Explain your answer.

....

....

....

[2]

5 A clothes shop has 112 shirts in stock.
On Monday it sells 17 shirts, and on Tuesday morning it gets a delivery of 38 shirts.
How many shirts does it have after the delivery arrives on Tuesday?

....

....

[2]

6   Matthew surveys 20 people in his class to find out how many siblings they have.
    His results are shown below.

    2   1   0   0   2   1   3   1   2   0

    2   2   0   1   1   0   1   2   0   1

(a) Complete the table.

Number of siblings	Tally	Frequency
0		
1		
2		
3		

[2]

(b) Write down the modal number of siblings.

    ....

[1]

(c) Draw a bar chart on the grid below to represent Matthew's results.

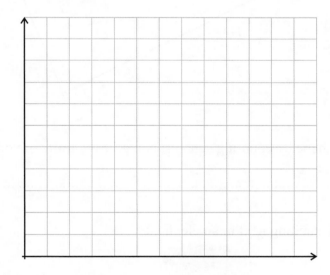

[4]

3

7   Use the words below to describe the likelihood of each of the events.

Impossible   Unlikely   Even   Likely   Certain

(a)   A card drawn at random from a pack of playing cards is a two of diamonds.

....

[1]

(b)   Christmas will fall in November next year.

....

[1]

(c)   When you roll a fair six-sided dice, it lands on an even number.

....

[1]

8   The shape below is drawn on a grid of centimetre squares.

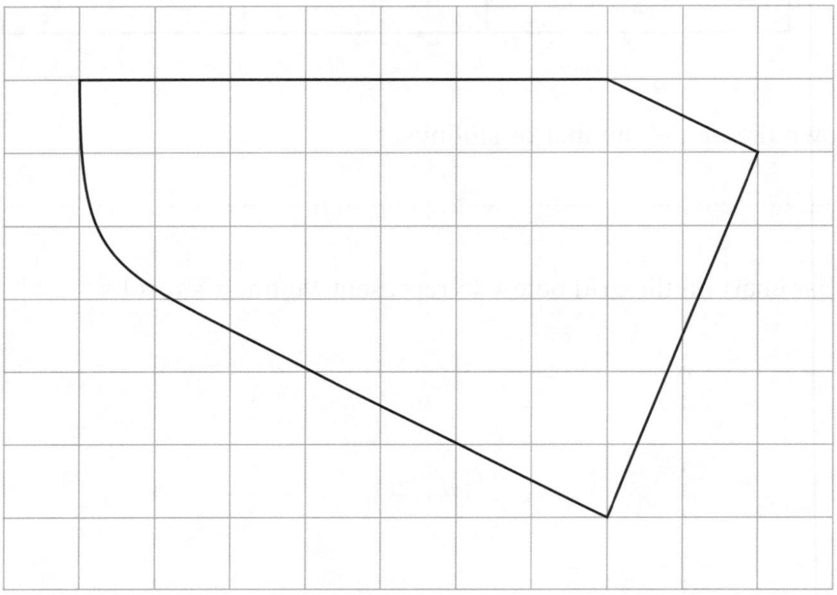

Estimate the area of the shape by counting squares, and give the **units** of your answer.

....

[3]

9   The picture shows a man standing next to an elephant.

Estimate the height of the elephant.

....

....

....

4

[3]

10 The table shows the temperatures in Glasgow and Barcelona at different times on the same day.

Time	Temperature in Glasgow (°C)	Temperature in Barcelona (°C)
04 00	−8	6
08 00	−2	9
12 00	3	15
16 00	1	14
20 00	−3	11

(a) Write down the maximum temperature across the two cities.

    ....

                                                                                                                            [1]

(b) How much colder was Glasgow than Barcelona at 08 00?

    ....

                                                                                                                            [2]

(c) What was the difference between the highest temperature in Glasgow
     and the lowest temperature in Barcelona?

    ....

    ....

                                                                                                                            [3]

11 The diagram below shows a circle with centre *O*.

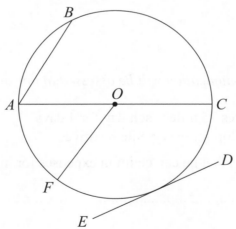

(a) Which straight line on the diagram represents a tangent of the circle?

                                                        .... [1]

(b) Write down a straight line from the diagram that represents a radius of the circle.

                                                        .... [1]

5

12 Arthur thinks of three different numbers. The numbers have a range of 6 and a mean of 5.
What are the three numbers?

....

....

[2]

13 For each of the statements below, choose a number from the list which matches the description.

19   125   36   18   84   32   124   48

(a) An even number less than 29.

....

[1]

(b) A power of 2.

....

[1]

(c) A square number.

....

[1]

(d) A cube number.

....

[1]

14 *The quality of your written communication will be assessed in this question.*

For work one week, Hassan drives 75 miles each day for 4 days.
He is able to claim in expenses 20p for every mile he drives.

Calculate the amount, in pounds, that he can claim in expenses for his working week.

....

....

....

....

....

....

[3]

6

15 Below is part of a bus timetable.

Windsor	08 12	08 46	09 08	09 33
Datchet	08 17	08 51	09 13	09 38
Old Windsor	08 23	08 57	09 19	09 44
Egham	08 33	09 07	09 29	09 54
Staines-upon-Thames	08 40	09 14	09 36	10 01
Chertsey	08 52	09 26	09 48	10 13
Weybridge	09 01	09 35	09 57	10 22

(a) (i) A bus leaves Datchet at 08 51.
What time should it arrive in Weybridge?

....

(ii) A later bus leaves Old Windsor at 09 44.
How long should it take to travel to Chertsey?

....

....

[3]

(b) Jake has a bus pass that gives him $\frac{1}{3}$ off the price of bus tickets.

He buys a return ticket from Windsor to Egham.
The normal price of the ticket is £3.60.

How much does Jake pay?

....

....

[2]

16 Work out the value of:

(a) $8 \times 2 + 7$

....

[1]

(b) 2^3

....

[1]

(c) $\sqrt{49}$

....

[1]

17 Below is a scale drawing of Sharon's kitchen.

(a) The shelves are 2 m long and 0.5 m wide. What is the scale of the drawing?

....

[1]

(b) What is the area of the real kitchen?

....

....

....

[3]

18 (a) Here are the first five terms of a number sequence.

   57   46   35   24   13

   (i) Write down the next number in the sequence.

   ....

   (ii) Explain how you found your answer.

   ....

   ....

   [2]

(b) The nth term of another sequence is given by $2n + 2$.
Find the 4th term of this sequence.

....

[1]

19 (a) Complete the table of values for $y = 2 + 2x$.

x	-1	0	1	2	3	4
y	0				8	10

[2]

(b) On the grid below, draw the graph of $y = 2 + 2x$.

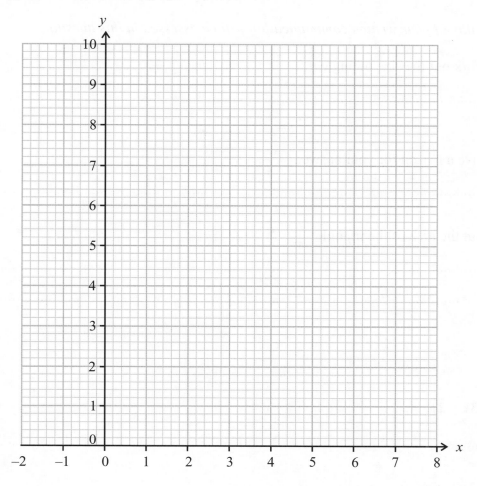

[2]

20 (a) Write down a prime number that is between 30 and 35.

....

[1]

(b) Write down all the factors of 28.

....

....

[2]

21 Here is a right-angled triangle.

50°

6 cm

Diagram not
accurately drawn

8 cm

(a) *The quality of your written communication will be assessed in this question.*

    (i) Work out the size of angle a.

    ....

$$a = \text{..................}^{\circ}$$

    (ii) Give a reason for your answer.

    ....

    [2]

(b) Work out the area of the triangle.

....

....

[2]

22 (a) Solve $3x = 21$

....

[1]

(b) Solve $2m + 5 = -9$

....

....

[2]

(c) Solve $5n - 11 = 2n + 4$

....

....

[2]

23 Robert is the conductor of a choir that is performing a concert for charity.

Robert needs to buy sheet music for each of the 40 singers in the choir.
A website offers the sheet music for £7.00 per copy
with a 10% discount for an order of 10 or more copies.
Robert also has to pay £318 to rent the venue for the concert.

Robert sells 95 tickets for the concert. A ticket for the concert costs £10.

Robert has agreed to donate 50% of the concert profits to charity.
How much money should he donate to charity?

....

....

....

....

....

....

....

[7]

24 A large supermarket chain is planning to open a new store in Digton.
Residents of Digton are asked to complete a questionnaire to give their views on the idea.

This is one of the questions from the questionnaire.

> There is nowhere in Digton that sells a good range of products, so
> Digton needs a new supermarket. Do you agree?
>
> ☐ Yes   ☐ Don't know

(a) Write down one thing that is wrong with this question.

....

....

[1]

(b) Design a more suitable question that could be used instead. Include some response boxes.

....

....

[2]

11

25 (a) Expand and simplify $3(2 + b) + 5(3 - b)$

....

....

[2]

(b) Factorise $6c - 8$

....

[1]

(c) Factorise fully $2d^2 + 10d$

....

....

[2]

26 *The quality of your written communication will be assessed in this question.*

A Youth Centre decides to organise a trip to a theme park.
They plan to hire a coach that costs £100 for the day.
The cost to get into the theme park is £15 per person.

The Youth Centre will charge £23 per person for the trip,
which includes the coach journey and entry to the theme park.

The trip can only go ahead if the Youth Centre makes enough money to cover its costs.
Work out how many people need to go on the trip for it to go ahead.

....

....

....

....

....

....

....

[4]

| Candidate Surname | | Candidate Forename(s) | |

| Centre Number | Candidate Number | Candidate Signature |

GCSE

Mathematics
Paper 2 (Calculator)

Foundation Tier

Practice Paper
Time allowed: 1 hour 45 minutes

You must have:
Pen, pencil, eraser, ruler, protractor, pair of compasses.
You may use tracing paper.

You **may use** a calculator.

Instructions to candidates
- Use **black** ink to write your answers.
- Write your name and other details in the spaces provided above.
- Answer **all** questions in the spaces provided.
- In calculations show clearly how you worked out your answers.
- Do all rough work on the paper.
- Unless a question tells you otherwise, take the value of π to be 3.142, or use the π button on your calculator.

Information for candidates
- The marks available are given in brackets at the end of each question.
- You may get marks for method, even if your answer is incorrect.
- There are 24 questions in this paper. There are no blank pages.
- There are 100 marks available for this paper.
- You will be assessed on the quality of your written communication in some questions. These will be clearly marked — take particular care here with spelling, punctuation and the quality of explanations.

Get the answers — on video and in print
Your free Online Edition of this book includes a link to step-by-step video solutions for this Exam Paper, plus worked solutions you can print out.
There's more info about how to get your Online Edition at the front of this book.

Answer ALL the questions.

Write your answers in the spaces provided.

You must show all of your working.

1 (a) Write twenty four thousand and twelve in digits.

....

[1]

(b) Put the following numbers in order of size, from smallest to largest.

85.3   95.3   85.03   90.9   87.2

.... , ... , ... , ... , ...

[1]

Jill has 4 cards, each with a number written on.

| 5 | 9 | 6 | 2 |

She lines all of the cards up to make a 4 digit number.

(c) (i) What is the largest number she can make?

....

(ii) What is the smallest number she can make?

....

[2]

2 The diagram below shows a quadrilateral.

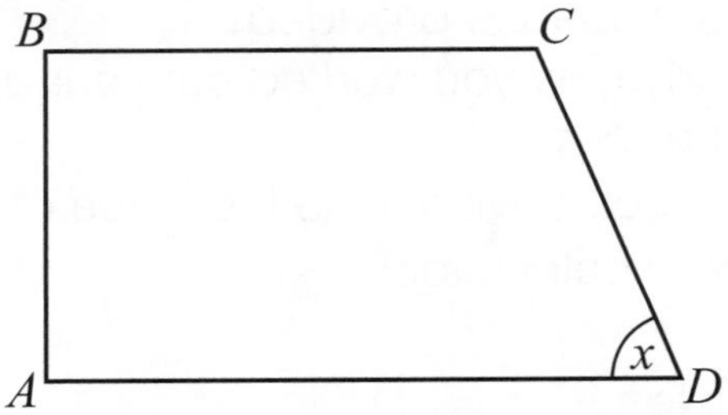

(a) Measure the length of *AB*.

....

[1]

(b) On the diagram, mark the midpoint of the line *AB* with a cross.

[1]

(c) Mark a right angle with the letter R.

[1]

(d) Give the mathematical name for the type of angle marked *x*.

....

[1]

3   (a)   Write down the fraction of this shape that is shaded.

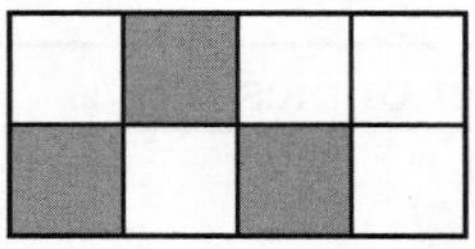

....

[1]

(b)   Write down the fraction of the shape that is shaded.
      Give your answer in its simplest form.

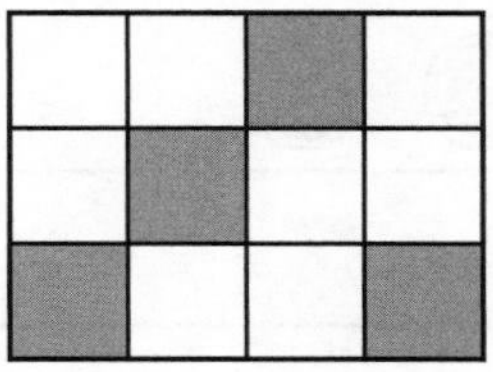

....

....

[2]

(c)   (i)   Shade 10% of this shape.

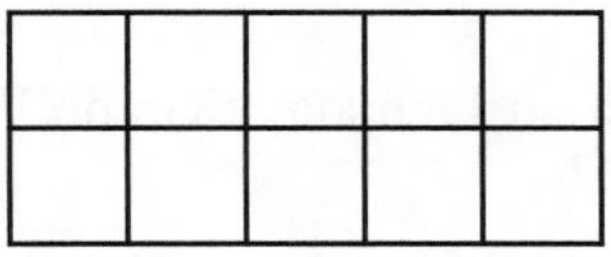

(ii)   Write down the proportion of the shape that is **not** shaded.
       Give your answer as a decimal.

....

....

[2]

2

4   The pictogram shows the number of pies eaten by customers at a restaurant one week.

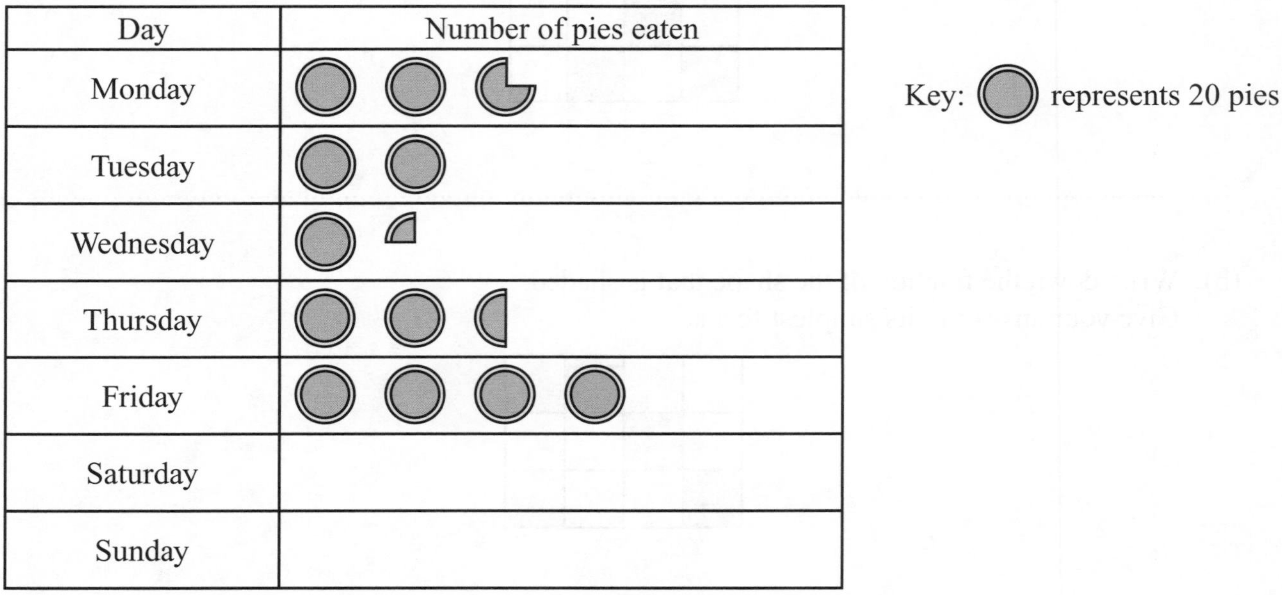

Day	Number of pies eaten
Monday	◯ ◯ ◗
Tuesday	◯ ◯
Wednesday	◯ ◸
Thursday	◯ ◯ ◖
Friday	◯ ◯ ◯ ◯
Saturday	
Sunday	

Key: ◯ represents 20 pies

(a) How many pies were eaten on Monday?

....

[1]

(b) How many more pies were eaten on Thursday than on Wednesday?

....

[1]

90 pies were eaten on Saturday.
35 pies were eaten on Sunday.

(c) Complete the pictogram using this information.

[2]

3

5   The table below gives some information about five candidates who have applied for a job as a postal worker.

	Driver's licence	At least grade G in GCSE Maths	Relevant work experience	Reference
Edward		✓		
Fiona	✓	✓		✓
Graham	✓		✓	✓
Nadia		✓		✓
Isaac		✓	✓	

(a)   Which candidates have at least a grade G in GCSE Maths?

....

[1]

(b)   Write down all the information from the table about Graham.

....

....

[1]

(c)   Write down the fraction of candidates who have relevant work experience.

....

[1]

6   (a)   Write down the number shown by the arrow.

....

[1]

(b)   Find the number 84 on the number line.
Mark it with an arrow.

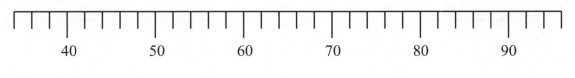

[1]

4

7 (a) Draw all of the lines of symmetry of this shape.

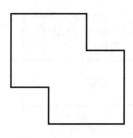

[1]

(b) Complete the pattern so that it has rotational symmetry of order 4 about the point O, by using the given shape to fill in the 3 empty sections of the grid.

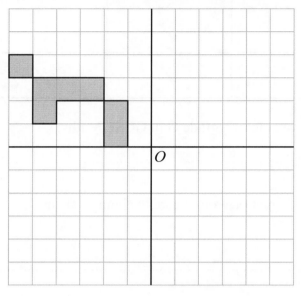

[3]

8 Jemma is the manager of a shoe shop.
One week Jemma recorded the size of each pair of a particular type of shoe that was sold.

Here are her results.

6   4   7   6   4   8   4

(a) Write down the modal size sold.

....

[1]

(b) Work out the median size sold.

....

[2]

(c) Explain why Jemma might be more interested in the modal size sold than the median size.

....

....

[1]

5

9 (a) Write down the mathematical name of each shape

(i) ....   (ii) ....

[2]

(b) Here is a 3D shape.

(i) Write down the number of faces of the shape.

....

(ii) Write down the number of edges of the shape.

....

[2]

10 Andrew runs a snack shop. These are the prices for some of the snacks he sells.

Price list	
Chocolate bar	£0.70
Crisps	£0.35
Flapjack	£0.95
Cereal bar	£1.10
Apple	£0.50

(a) How much does it cost to buy a chocolate bar, a cereal bar and a flapjack?

....

[1]

(b) A customer buys two packets of crisps and an apple. They pay with a £5 note.
How much change should Andrew give them?

....

....

[2]

(c) Next week, Andrew is going to put all of his prices up by 20%.
How much will it cost to buy a cereal bar and an apple next week?

....

....

....

[3]

6

11 Look at the coordinate grid.

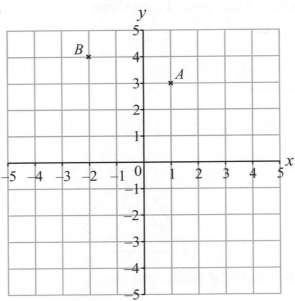

(a) Write down the coordinates of point A.

....

[1]

(b) Write down the coordinates of point B.

....

[1]

(c) Plot the point $(-3, -4)$ on the grid. Label this point C.

[1]

12 Hamish wants to switch gas suppliers. His two options are shown below.

Energy Save	
Fixed charge	4p per unit

Smart Energy	
First 500 units	5p per unit
Additional units	2p per unit

Hamish checks his meter readings.

New reading: 4638 units
Old reading: 3512 units

Work out which supplier he should choose.

....

....

....

....

....

....

[6]

13

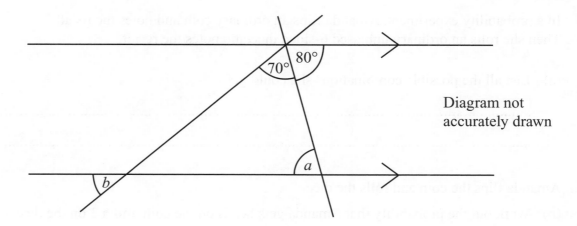

Diagram not accurately drawn

(a) Write down the size of angle *a* and give a reason for your answer.

....

[2]

(b) Work out the size of angle *b*.

....

$$b = \text{.................}°$$

[2]

14 Mark is following a recipe for roasting a chicken.
The recipe gives the following information on the cooking time for a chicken:

> *"Cook the chicken for 50 minutes per kg, plus an extra 20 minutes."*

(a) Mark has bought a chicken that weighs 2.4 kg.
Calculate how long he should cook the chicken for.

....

....

[2]

Mark is also making a salad to go with his chicken.

> **Salad Dressing: Serves 4**
> 3 tablespoons olive oil
> 1 tablespoon vinegar
> Seasoning

(b) Mark wants to make a salad dressing for six people using the recipe above.
How much olive oil should he use?

....

[1]

8

15 In a probability experiment, Amanda flips an ordinary coin and notes the result.
Then she rolls an ordinary unbiased 6-sided dice and notes the result.

(a) List all the possible combinations she could get.

....

....

[2]

Amanda flips the coin and rolls the dice.

(b) Work out the probability that Amanda gets heads on the coin **and** a 3 on the dice.

....

....

[1]

(c) Work out the probability that she gets heads on the coin **and** a 3 or higher on the dice.
Give your answer as a fraction in its simplest form.

....

....

[2]

16 $e = 3, f = 5$ and $g = -7$

Find the value of

(a) $e^2 + g^2$

....

....

[2]

(b) $\dfrac{efg}{2}$

....

....

[2]

17 The graph below can be used to convert between pounds (£) and euros (€).

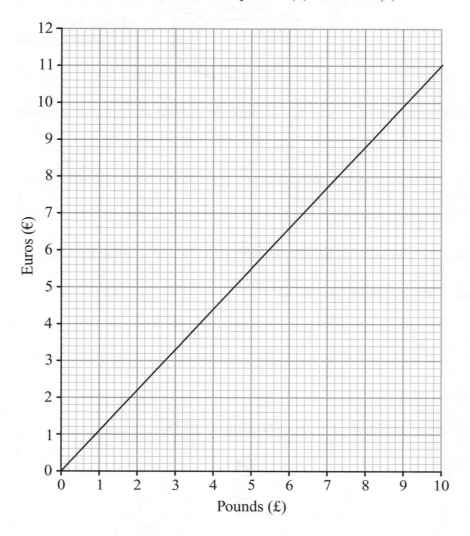

(a) Use the graph to convert £2 to euros.

....

[1]

(b) Use the graph to convert €3 to pounds.

....

[1]

(c) Use the graph to work out how much £20 is in euros.

....

....

[2]

18 The diagram shows a cuboid.

2.8 cm

Diagram not
accurately drawn

3.7 cm

4.9 cm

(a) Calculate the volume of the cuboid. Include the correct units in your answer.

....

....

....

[3]

Another cuboid has a volume of 56 cm³, a width of 4 cm and a length of 7 cm.

(b) Calculate h, the height of the cuboid.

....

....

[2]

19 (a) Reflect shape **A** in the line $x = 1$. Label your shape **B**.

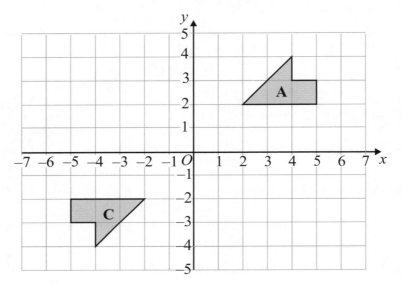

[2]

(b) Describe fully the single transformation that maps shape **C** onto shape **A**.

....

....

....

[3]

11

20 A painter wants to calculate the cost of painting the four outside walls of a warehouse.
The diagram below gives the dimensions of the warehouse.

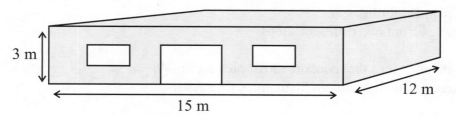

Diagram not
accurately drawn

3 m

15 m

12 m

There are 5 windows in the warehouse that each measure 2 m by 1 m and
a door that measures 3 m by 2.5 m.

The paint covers 13 m² per litre.
The paint can be bought in tins that contain 5 litres or 2.5 litres.
5 litre tins cost £20.99
2.5 litre tins cost £12.99

Calculate the cheapest price for painting the warehouse. You must show all your working.

....

....

....

....

....

....

....

....

[6]

21 The equation $x^3 - x - 4 = 0$ has a solution between 1 and 2.

Use trial and improvement to find this solution.
Give your answer correct to one decimal place.

You must show **ALL** of your working.

....

....

....

....

....

....

[4]

22 *The quality of your written communication will be assessed in this question.*

Tom is buying nappies for his son.
He can buy nappies from two different shops.

Shop A sells medium packs that contain 32 nappies for £6.40,
Shop B sells large packs that contain 56 nappies for £7.84.

Tom has a voucher that gives him 25% off the price of nappies at shop A.

Should Tom buy the nappies at shop A or shop B?
You must show all your working.

....

....

....

....

....

....

....

....

....

....

[4]

23 Simplify:
   (a) $a^4 \times a^5$

   ....

[1]

   (b) $b^9 \div b^3$

   ....

[1]

24 (a) The diagram shows a right-angled triangle.

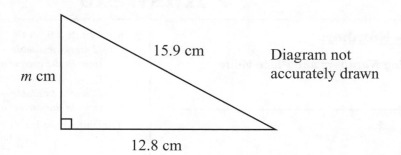

15.9 cm

m cm

Diagram not accurately drawn

12.8 cm

Calculate the value of *m*. Give your answer correct to 1 decimal place.

....

....

[2]

(b) *The quality of your written communication will be assessed in this question.*

Explain why triangle *ABC* below cannot be a right-angled triangle.

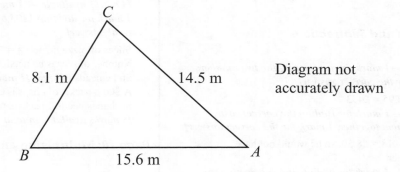

C

8.1 m

14.5 m

Diagram not accurately drawn

B

15.6 m

A

....

....

....

....

....

[3]

Answers

Section One — Numbers

Pages 4-5: Ordering Numbers and Place Value

1. a) 58 *[1 mark]*
   b) 530 *[1 mark]*
   c)
   [1 mark]

2. a) Five thousand and seventy-nine *[1 mark]*
   b) 6105 *[1 mark]*
   c) 90/ninety *[1 mark]*

3. a) Twenty-six thousand and four *[1 mark]*
   b) 20 364 *[1 mark]*
   c) 800/eight hundred *[1 mark]*

4. a) Four hundred and twenty thousand, four hundred
      and fifty-seven *[1 mark]*
   b) 6 000 000 *[1 mark]*
   c) 2000/two thousand *[1 mark]*

5. 98 649, 98 653, 100 003, 100 010 *[1 mark]*

6. 53.3, 52.91, 35.6, 35.54, 35.06 *[1 mark]*

7. a) 12 478 *[1 mark]*
   b) 87 421 *[1 mark]*

Pages 6-7: Addition and Subtraction

1. $522 - (197 + 24) = 301$
   *[2 marks available — 1 mark for subtracting the two numbers
   from 522, 1 mark for the correct answer]*

2. £290 + £59 + £39 + £95 = £483
   *[3 marks available — 1 mark for finding the correct costs,
   1 mark for adding them together, 1 mark for the correct answer]*

3. £15 − £8.50 + £20 − £18 = £8.50, so he would not have
   £10 to give to his sister.
   *[2 marks available — 1 mark for adding and subtracting the
   correct amounts to work out how much he would have left,
   1 mark for the correct conclusion]*

4. 17.3 − 5.54 = 11.76 *[1 mark]*

5. Total cost = £2.15 + £2.40 + £2.40 = £6.95
   Change = £10 − £6.95 = £3.05
   *[2 marks available — 1 mark for adding amounts and
   subtracting from £10, 1 mark for the correct answer]*

6. £3.40 + £2.30 + £1.40 + £1.50 = £8.60
   £10 − £8.60 = £1.40
   *[3 marks available — 1 mark for finding the correct costs,
   1 mark for adding them together and subtracting from £10,
   1 mark for the correct answer]*

Page 8-9: Multiplying and Dividing Without a Calculator

1. a)
   $$\begin{array}{r} 113 \\ \times\ 76 \\ \hline 678 \\ +\ 7910 \\ \hline 8588 \end{array}$$
   *[2 marks available — 1 mark for a correct method,
   1 mark for the correct answer]*
   "A correct method" here can be any non-calculator
   multiplication method.

   b)
   $$\begin{array}{r} 376 \\ \times\ 48 \\ \hline 3008 \\ +\ 15040 \\ \hline 18048 \end{array}$$
   *[2 marks available — 1 mark for a correct method,
   1 mark for the correct answer]*

2. a) $19 + 26 \div 2 = 19 + 13 = 32$
   *[2 marks available — 1 mark for doing the calculation
   steps in the correct order, 1 mark for the correct answer]*
   b) $(22 - 18) \times (3 + 8) = 4 \times 11 = 44$
   *[2 marks available — 1 mark for doing the calculation
   steps in the correct order, 1 mark for the correct answer]*

3. Total miles travelled = $(30 \times 2) + (28 \times 2) + (39 \times 2) + (40 \times 2)$
   $= 60 + 56 + 78 + 80$
   $= 274$ miles
   Expenses for miles travelled = 274 × 30p = 8220p = £82.20
   Expenses for food = 4 × £8 = £32
   Total expenses = £82.20 + £32 = £114.20
   *[5 marks available — 1 mark for multiplying the distances by 2,
   1 mark for finding total miles, 1 mark for multiplying total
   miles by 30 or 0.3(0), 1 mark for finding food expenses,
   1 mark for the correct final answer]*

4. Number of bunches = $\dfrac{10}{1.85} \approx \dfrac{10}{2} = 5$
   *[2 marks available — 1 mark for rounding up 1.85 to 2,
   1 mark for the correct final answer]*

5. £200 − £5 = £195
   $15\overline{)19^4 5}$, so each ticket costs £13
   *[3 marks available — 1 mark for subtracting £5 from £200,
   1 mark for dividing £195 by 15, 1 mark for the correct
   final answer]*

6. Slices of pizza he needs = 15 × 3 = 45 *[1 mark]*
   Number of pizzas he needs = 45 ÷ 8 *[1 mark]* = 5.625
   So he needs 6 pizzas *[1 mark]*
   A 300 g packet of crisps is enough for 300 ÷ 25 = 12 people *[1 mark]*
   So James needs 2 packets of crisps *[1 mark]*
   [5 marks available in total — as above]

Page 10: Multiplying and Dividing with Decimals

1. a)
   $$\begin{array}{r} 16 \\ \times\ 7 \\ \hline 112 \end{array}$$
   16 × 0.7 has one digit after the decimal point,
   so 16 × 0.7 = 11.2
   *[2 marks available — 1 mark for a correct method,
   1 mark for the correct answer]*
   "A correct method" can be any non-calculator multiplication method.

   b)
   $$\begin{array}{r} 25 \\ \times\ 19 \\ \hline 225 \\ +\ 250 \\ \hline 475 \end{array}$$
   25 × 1.9 has one digit after the decimal point,
   so 25 × 1.9 = 47.5
   *[2 marks available — 1 mark for a correct method,
   1 mark for the correct answer]*

2. a) $5.6 \times 4.27 = (23\ 912 \div 10) \div 100 = 23.912$ *[1 mark]*
   b) $0.56 \times 4\ 270\ 000 = (23\ 912 \div 100) \times 10\ 000 = 2\ 391\ 200$
   [1 mark]
   c) $2391.2 \div 4.27 = (56 \div 10) \times 100 = 560$ *[1 mark]*

3. $7 \times 8 = 56$
   0.7 × 0.8 has two digits after the decimal point,
   so 0.7 × 0.8 = 0.56
   *[2 marks available — 1 mark for a correct method,
   1 mark for the correct answer]*

4. a) $14 \div 0.7 = \dfrac{14}{0.7} = \dfrac{140}{7} = 20$
   *[2 marks available — 1 mark for a correct method,
   1 mark for the correct answer]*
   b) $23 \div 0.46 = \dfrac{23}{0.46} = \dfrac{2300}{46} = 50$
   *[2 marks available — 1 mark for a correct method,
   1 mark for the correct answer]*

Page 11: Negative Numbers

1   −103.1, −102.7, −102.4, −99.8 , −98.9, 98.9, 99.5 *[1 mark]*

2 a) 9 − 4 = 5 °C *[1 mark]*

   b) St Petersburg *[1 mark]*

   c) 22 − (−8) = 30 °C
      [3 marks available — 1 mark for finding the correct values, 1 mark for subtracting, 1 mark for the correct answer]

3 a) −11 × 7 = −77 *[1 mark]*

   b) −72 ÷ −8 = 9 *[1 mark]*

Page 12: Special Types of Number

1 a) 41 *[1 mark]*

   b) 100 *[1 mark]*

   c) 27 *[1 mark]*

2 a) 81 *[1 mark]*

   b) 64 *[1 mark]*

   c) 6 *[1 mark]*

Page 13: Prime Numbers, Multiples and Factors

1 a) 7 or 11 *[1 mark for either]*

   b) 15 *[1 mark]*

   c) 15 *[1 mark]*

   d) 1 and 12, or 7 and 12, or 11 and 12
      [1 mark available — 1 mark maximum for any of the three options above]

2 a) 1, 2, 4, 5, 10, 20
      [2 marks available — 2 marks if all 6 factors are correct and no extra incorrect factors have been included, otherwise 1 mark if all 6 factors are correct but 1 extra incorrect factor has been included, or if at least 4 factors are correct and there are no more than 6 numbers listed in total]

   b) 56, 64 *[1 mark]*

3 a) E.g. 21, 42 *[1 mark for any two multiples of 21]*

   b) 47 *[1 mark]*

Page 14: Prime Factors, LCM and HCF

1 a)

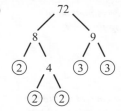

    72 = 2 × 2 × 2 × 3 × 3 = $2^3 × 3^2$
    [3 marks available — 1 mark for a correct method, 1 mark for all prime factors correct, 1 mark for answer in index form]

   b) Factors of 54 are: 1, 2, 3, 6, 9, ⑱, 27, 54
      Factors of 72 are: 1, 2, 3, 4, 6, 8, 9, 12, ⑱, 24, 36, 72

      So the highest common factor (HCF) is 18 *[1 mark]*
      You could use the prime factors to go straight to finding the HCF, but there's a good chance of making a mistake. It's much safer to list all the factors and find the HCF that way, even if it takes a bit longer.

2 E.g. prime factors of 84:

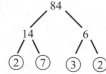

    84 = 2 × 2 × 3 × 7 = $2^2 × 3 × 7$
    So HCF of 84 and 132 = $2^2 × 3$ = 12
    [3 marks available — 1 mark for a correct method of finding the prime factors of 84, 1 mark for all correct prime factors of 84, 1 mark for correct HCF of 84 and 132]

3 Multiples of 35 are: 35, 70, 105, 140, 175, 210, 245, 280, 315, 350, ㊟385, 420, ...
   Multiples of 55 are: 55, 110, 165, 220, 275, 330, ㊟385, 440, ...

   So the LCM is 385, which is the minimum number of jars he needs.

   So the minimum number of packs he needs is 385 ÷ 35 = 11 packs
   [3 marks available — 1 mark for a correct method to find LCM, 1 mark for LCM correct, 1 mark for correct number of packs]

Page 15: Fractions, Decimals and Percentages

1 a) $\frac{3}{4}$ = 3 ÷ 4 = 0.75 *[1 mark]*

   b) 0.06 × 100 = 6% *[1 mark]*

   c) 35% = $\frac{35}{100}$ *[1 mark]*
       = $\frac{35 ÷ 5}{100 ÷ 5} = \frac{7}{20}$ *[1 mark]*
      [2 marks available in total — as above]

2 a) 14 ÷ 20 = 0.7 *[1 mark]*
      0.7 × 100 = 70% *[1 mark]*
      [2 marks available in total — as above]
      Or you could multiply the top and bottom of the fraction by 5 to give $\frac{70}{100}$ = 70%.

   b) 85% = $\frac{85}{100}$ *[1 mark]*
       = $\frac{85 ÷ 5}{100 ÷ 5} = \frac{17}{20}$ *[1 mark]*
      [2 marks available in total — as above]

3 a) 80% = 80 ÷ 100 = 0.8 *[1 mark]*

   b) $\frac{5}{8}$ = 5 ÷ 8 = 0.625 *[1 mark]*

   c) $\frac{5}{8}$, 0.65, 80% *[1 mark]*

Page 16: Equivalent Fractions

1 a) $\frac{12 ÷ 6}{30 ÷ 6} = \frac{2}{5}$ *[1 mark]*

   b) 18 shaded squares out of 50, so $\frac{18}{50} = \frac{9}{25}$
      [2 marks available — 2 marks for the correct final answer, otherwise 1 mark for a correct equivalent fraction]

   c) E.g.

      [1 mark for any 40 squares shaded]

2 a) $\frac{18}{7} = 2\frac{4}{7}$ *[1 mark]*

   b) $1\frac{3}{4} = \frac{4+3}{4} = \frac{7}{4}$ *[1 mark]*

3 a) $\frac{3}{12} = \frac{1}{4} \neq \frac{1}{3}$ and $\frac{6}{20} = \frac{3}{10} \neq \frac{3}{9} = \frac{1}{3}$
      So $\frac{3}{12}$ and $\frac{6}{20}$
      [2 marks available — 1 mark for each correct answer]

   b) $\frac{4}{5} = \frac{36}{45}, \frac{7}{9} = \frac{35}{45}, \frac{13}{15} = \frac{39}{45}$
      So the largest fraction is $\frac{13}{15}$
      [3 marks available — 1 mark for attempting to convert to equivalent fractions or to draw shaded diagrams, 1 mark if these are correct, 1 mark for the correct conclusion]

Pages 17-18: Fractions

1 a) $\frac{1}{2} × \frac{1}{6} = \frac{1×1}{2×6} = \frac{1}{12}$ *[1 mark]*

   b) $\frac{2}{3} ÷ \frac{3}{5} = \frac{2}{3} × \frac{5}{3} = \frac{2×5}{3×3} = \frac{10}{9}$ or $1\frac{1}{9}$
      [2 marks available — 1 mark for changing to the reciprocal fraction and multiplying, 1 mark for the correct answer]

2 a) $\dfrac{3}{4} \times \dfrac{2}{5} = \dfrac{3 \times 2}{4 \times 5} = \dfrac{6}{20} = \dfrac{3}{10}$
[2 marks available — 1 mark for multiplying the fractions, 1 mark for the final answer in its simplest form]

b) $9)\overline{2.^{2}0^{2}0^{2}0...}$ $0.2\ 2\ 2...$

So $\dfrac{2}{9} = 0.222... = 0.\dot{2}$
[3 marks available — 1 mark for using a division method, 1 mark for 0.22..., 1 mark for the correct final answer]

3 a) $\dfrac{1}{6} + \dfrac{2}{3} = \dfrac{1}{6} + \dfrac{4}{6} = \dfrac{1+4}{6} = \dfrac{5}{6}$
[2 marks available — 1 mark for finding a common denominator, 1 mark for the correct answer]

b) $\dfrac{7}{8} - \dfrac{3}{4} = \dfrac{7}{8} - \dfrac{6}{8} = \dfrac{7-6}{8} = \dfrac{1}{8}$
[2 marks available — 1 mark for finding a common denominator, 1 mark for the correct answer]

4 a) $\dfrac{1}{3} + \dfrac{2}{5} = \dfrac{5}{15} + \dfrac{6}{15} = \dfrac{5+6}{15} = \dfrac{11}{15}$
[2 marks available — 1 mark for finding a common denominator, 1 mark for the correct answer]

b) $\dfrac{1}{2} - \dfrac{2}{7} = \dfrac{7}{14} - \dfrac{4}{14} = \dfrac{7-4}{14} = \dfrac{3}{14}$
[2 marks available — 1 mark for finding a common denominator, 1 mark for the correct answer]

5 a) $(60 \div 5) \times 3 = 12 \times 3 = 36$
[2 marks available — 1 mark for dividing by 5, 1 mark for the correct answer]
You could also multiply 60 by 0.6.

b) $\dfrac{15}{40} = \dfrac{3}{8}$
[2 marks available — 1 mark for putting the numbers into a fraction, 1 mark for the correct final answer]

6 Calculate the total cost if he pays in full today:
£1100 ÷ 4 = £275, £1100 − £275 = £825
Calculate the total cost if he pays £150 today, then 12 monthly payments of £55:
£150 + (12 × £55) = £150 + £660 = £810
So the cheaper way for Chris to pay for the car is by paying £150 today, followed by 12 monthly payments of £55.
[4 marks available — 1 mark for the correct method to find the total cost if he pays in full today, 1 mark for the correct method to find the total cost if he pays £150 then 12 monthly payments, 1 mark if both of these values are correct, 1 mark for the correct conclusion from your values]

7 7 *[1 mark]*

8 $12 \times \dfrac{2}{5} = \dfrac{24}{5}$ *[1 mark]*

$\dfrac{24}{5} = 4\dfrac{4}{5}$ *[1 mark]*

Sarah will need to order 5 pizzas. *[1 mark]*
[3 marks available in total — as above]
Remember to round up — 4 pizzas wouldn't be enough.

Pages 19-20: Proportion Problems

1 Price per ml:
250 ml bottle: £2.30 ÷ 250 = £0.0092
330 ml bottle: £2.97 ÷ 330 = £0.009
500 ml bottle: £4.10 ÷ 500 = £0.0082
Therefore the 500 ml bottle is the best value for money.
[2 marks available — 1 mark for finding the price per ml, 1 mark for the correct answer]

2 Flour: (175 ÷ 20) × 70 = 612.5 g
Butter: (175 ÷ 20) × 70 = 612.5 g
Sugar: (120 ÷ 20) × 70 = 420 g
Baking powder: (2.5 ÷ 20) × 70 = 8.75 tsp
Eggs: (4 ÷ 20) × 70 = 14
[3 marks available — 1 mark for dividing each quantity by 20, 1 mark for multiplying each of these by 70, 1 mark if all 5 final answers are correct]

3 Cost of broccoli = 8.6 × £1.35 = £11.61 *[1 mark]*
Cost of custard powder = £46.71 − £11.61 = £35.10 *[1 mark]*
Cost of 1 tin of custard powder = £35.10 ÷ 13 *[1 mark]*
 = £2.70 *[1 mark]*
[4 marks available in total — as above]

4 a) Euros = 275 × 1.15 *[1 mark]*
 = €316.25 *[1 mark]*
[2 marks available in total — as above]

b) Pounds = 60 ÷ 1.25 *[1 mark]*
 = £48.00 *[1 mark]*
[2 marks available in total — as above]

5 Number of man-hours to build section = 25 × 48 *[1 mark]*
 = 1200 *[1 mark]*
Number of hours to build section with 16 men = 1200 ÷ 16 *[1 mark]*
 = 75 hours *[1 mark]*
[4 marks available in total — as above]

Pages 21-23: Percentages

1 100% = £450
10% = £450 ÷ 10 = £45
60% = £45 × 6 = £270
[2 marks available — 1 mark for a correct method, 1 mark for the correct final answer]

2 50 − 35 = 15 *[1 mark]*
$\dfrac{15}{50} \times 100$ *[1 mark]*
= 30% *[1 mark]*
[3 marks available in total — as above]

3 a) 10% = 10 ÷ 100 = 0.1
10% of £18 = 0.1 × £18 = £1.80
[2 marks available — 1 mark for a correct method, 1 mark for the correct answer]

b) (£6 ÷ £24) × 100 = 0.25 × 100 = 25%
[2 marks available — 1 mark for a correct method, 1 mark for the correct answer]

4 3% = 3 ÷ 100 = 0.03
3% of £200 = 0.03 × £200 = £6
4 × £6 = £24
[3 marks available — 1 mark for a correct method to find 3% of £200, 1 mark for multiplying this by 4, 1 mark for the correct answer]

5 a) 20% = 20 ÷ 100 = 0.2
20% of £33.25 = 0.2 × £33.25 = £6.65
£33.25 + £6.65 = £39.90
[3 marks available — 1 mark for a correct method to find 20% of £33.25, 1 mark for adding this to £33.25, 1 mark for the correct answer]
You could multiply by 1.2 instead of multiplying by 0.2 and adding.

b) (£6.38 ÷ £29) × 100 = 0.22 × 100 = 22%
[2 marks available — 1 mark for a correct method, 1 mark for the correct answer]

c) £200 − £175 = £25 *[1 mark]*
(£25 ÷ £200) × 100 *[1 mark]*
= 12.5% *[1 mark]*
[3 marks available in total — as above]

6 Deposit: 12% = 12 ÷ 100 = 0.12
 12% of £750 = £750 × 0.12 = £90 *[1 mark]*
Total of monthly payments = 18 × 44 = £792 *[1 mark]*
Total cost = 90 + 792 = £882 *[1 mark]*
[3 marks available in total — as above]

7 $£120\,000 \times \left(1 + \dfrac{15}{100}\right)^{5} = £241\,362.86... = £241\,000$ (to nearest £1000)
[3 marks available — 1 mark for using correct formula, 2 marks for correct answer to nearest £1000, otherwise 1 mark for an unrounded answer]

Answers

8 £16 000 – £9440 = £6560 *[1 mark]*
   20% = 20 ÷ 100 = 0.2
   20% of £6560 = 0.2 × £6560 *[1 mark]*
   = £1312 *[1 mark]*
   [3 marks available in total — as above]

9 11% = 11 ÷ 100 = 0.11
   Multiplier = 1 – 0.11 = 0.89
   Value after 1 year = £21 500 × 0.89 = £19 135
   Value after 2 years = £19 135 × 0.89 = £17 030.15
   [3 marks available — 1 mark for a method to find 11%, 1 mark for subtracting 11% twice, 1 mark for correct final answer]

10 Total spent per computer = £50 + £20 = £70 *[1 mark]*
   40% = 40 ÷ 100 = 0.4
   40% of total spent on each computer = 0.4 × £70 = £28
   So the selling price for the first 12 computers is:
   £70 + £28 *[1 mark]*
   = £98 *[1 mark]*
   12 × £98 = £1176 *[1 mark]*
   12% = 12 ÷ 100 = 0.12
   12% of selling price = 0.12 × £98 = £11.76
   So the new selling price is:
   £98 – £11.76 *[1 mark]*
   = £86.24 *[1 mark]*
   8 × £86.24 = £689.92 *[1 mark]*
   Total profit/loss = £1176 + £689.92 – (20 × £70)
   = £1865.92 – £1400 = £465.92
   So John made an overall profit of £465.92 *[1 mark]*
   [8 marks available in total — as above]
   If you've used a different method, but you've shown all your working and got the correct final answer, give yourself full marks.

Pages 24-25: Ratios

1 $\div 4 \left(\begin{array}{c} 4:12 \\ 1:3 \end{array} \right) \div 4$
   [1 mark]

2 a) boys : girls
       = 12 : 14
       =   6 : 7 *[1 mark]*
   b) 25 ÷ (2 + 3) = 5 *[1 mark]*
       Number of girls is 5 × 3 = 15 *[1 mark]*
       [2 marks available in total — as above]

3 700 ÷ (4 + 3 + 7) = 700 ÷ 14
   = 50 ml
   Orange juice: 50 × 4 = 200 ml
   Pineapple juice : 50 × 3 = 150 ml
   Lemonade: 50 × 7 = 350 ml
   [3 marks available — 1 mark for dividing 700 by the sum of the numbers in the ratio, 1 mark for multiplying this number by each number in the ratio, 1 mark if all three quantities are correct]

4 £160 ÷ (3 + 6 + 7) = £160 ÷ 16 *[1 mark]*
   = £10
   So Christine's share = £10 × 7 = £70 *[1 mark]*
   [2 marks available in total — as above]

5 Feed for Elmo:
   Weight of oats = 5 ÷ (5 + 6 + 5) × 1600 = 500 g
   Weight of sunflower seeds = 6 ÷ (5 + 6 + 5) × 1600 = 600 g
   Weight of sesame seeds = 5 ÷ (5 + 6 + 5) × 1600 = 500 g
   Cost of oats = 1.80 × (500 ÷ 1000) = £0.90
   Cost of sunflower seeds = 6.00 × (600 ÷ 1000) = £3.60
   Cost of sesame seeds = 4.50 × (500 ÷ 1000) = £2.25

   Feed for Ziggy:
   Weight of oats = 8 ÷ (8 + 1 + 3) × 1200 = 800 g
   Weight of sunflower seeds = 1 ÷ (8 + 1 + 3) × 1200 = 100 g
   Weight of sesame seeds = 3 ÷ (8 + 1 + 3) × 1200 = 300 g
   Cost of oats = 1.80 × (800 ÷ 1000) = £1.44
   Cost of sunflower seeds = 6.00 × (100 ÷ 1000) = £0.60
   Cost of sesame seeds = 4.50 × (300 ÷ 1000) = £1.35

   Total cost = 0.90 + 3.60 + 2.25 + 1.44 + 0.60 + 1.35 = £10.14

[5 marks available — 1 mark for calculating the weight of at least 1 ingredient of Elmo's feed, 1 mark for calculating the weight of at least 1 ingredient of Ziggy's feed, 1 mark for calculating the cost of at least 1 ingredient of Elmo's feed, 1 mark for calculating the cost of at least 1 ingredient of Ziggy's feed, 1 mark for the correct final answer]

Page 26: Calculating Bills

1 a)

ITEM	COST
4 tubes of red paint (£1.79 per tube)	£7.16
3 tubes of blue paint (£1.99 per tube)	£5.97
2 paintbrushes (£7.49 each)	£14.98
1 easel	£69.99
TOTAL	£98.10

   [4 marks available — 1 mark for each correct value]
   b) 20% = 20 ÷ 100 = 0.2
       Saving = £98.10 × 0.2 = £19.62 *[1 mark]*

2 Number of units used = 44439 – 43202 = 1237 *[1 mark]*
   Cost of first 100 units = 100 × 0.12 = £12 *[1 mark]*
   Cost of remaining units = (1237 – 100) × 0.16 = £181.92 *[1 mark]*
   Total bill = £12 + £181.92 + £37.25 = £231.17 *[1 mark]*
   Total already paid = £135 + £25 = £160 *[1 mark]*
   Total left on bill = £231.17 – £160 = £71.17 *[1 mark]*
   [6 marks available in total — as above]

Page 27: Rounding Off and Estimating Calculations

1 a) 120 *[1 mark]*
   b) 2600 *[1 mark]*
   c) 500 000 *[1 mark]*

2 a) 428.6 light years *[1 mark]*
   b) 430 light years *[1 mark]*

3 $\dfrac{4.32^2 - \sqrt{13.4}}{16.3 + 2.19}$ = 0.8113466... *[1 mark]*
   = 0.811 *[1 mark]*
   [2 marks available in total — as above]

4 E.g. $\dfrac{12.2 \times 1.86}{0.19} \approx \dfrac{10 \times 2}{0.2} = \dfrac{20}{0.2} = 100$
   [3 marks available — 1 mark for rounding to suitable values, 1 mark for next calculation step, 1 mark for the correct final answer using your values]

Page 28: Powers and Roots

1 a) 8.7^3 = 658.503 *[1 mark]*
   b) $\sqrt{2025}$ = 45 *[1 mark]*

2 Since 6^2 = 36 and 7^2 = 49, $6 < \sqrt{42} < 7$
   So, $\sqrt{42} \approx 6.5$ *[1 mark]*
   You would be given the mark here for any answer which was greater than 6 and less than 7.

3 a) $6^{(4 + 7)} = 6^{11}$ *[1 mark]*
   b) $6^{(5 - 3)} = 6^2$ *[1 mark]*

4 $\dfrac{3^4 \times 3^7}{3^6} = \dfrac{3^{(4+7)}}{3^6} = \dfrac{3^{11}}{3^6} = 3^{(11-6)} = 3^5$
   [2 marks available — 1 mark for a correct attempt at adding or subtracting powers, 1 mark for the correct final answer]

Section Two — Algebra

Page 29: Simplifying Terms

1 a) 4p *[1 mark]*
   b) 2m *[1 mark]*
   c) 4p + 3r
       [2 marks available — 1 mark for 4p and 1 mark for 3r]

2 a) w^5 *[1 mark]*

   b) $x^{(9-3)} = x^6$ *[1 mark]*

   c) y^5 *[1 mark]*
      Remember — if you're multiplying, you add the powers.

3 a) $10ab$ *[1 mark]*

   b) $x^2 \times x^4 = x^{(2+4)} = x^6$ *[1 mark]*
      $x^8 \div x^6 = x^{(8-6)} = x^2$ *[1 mark]*
      [2 marks available in total — as above]

   c) $25p^{(3 \times 2)} = 25p^6$
      [2 marks available — 1 mark for 25 and 1 mark for p^6]

Page 30: Multiplying Out Brackets and Common Factors

1 a) $3(x - 2)$
      $= (3 \times x) + (3 \times -2)$
      $= 3x - 6$ *[1 mark]*

   b) $x(x + 4)$
      $= (x \times x) + (x \times 4)$
      $= x^2 + 4x$ *[1 mark]*

2 a) $5(x + y)$
      $= (5 \times x) + (5 \times y)$
      $= 5x + 5y$ *[1 mark]*

   b) $s(2s - 3)$
      $= (s \times 2s) + (s \times -3)$
      $= 2s^2 - 3s$ *[1 mark]*

3 $3(x - 1) + 5(x + 2)$
   $= (3 \times x) + (3 \times -1) + (5 \times x) + (5 \times 2)$
   $= 3x - 3 + 5x + 10$ *[1 mark]*
   $= 8x + 7$ *[1 mark]*
   [2 marks available in total — as above]

4 a) $6x + 3 = (3 \times 2x) + (3 \times 1) = 3(2x + 1)$ *[1 mark]*

   b) $x(x + 7)$ *[1 mark]*

   c) $5(5p - 3q)$ *[1 mark]*

Pages 31-32: Solving Equations

1 a) $x + 3 = 12$
      $x = 12 - 3 = 9$ *[1 mark]*

   b) $6x = 24$
      $x = 24 \div 6 = 4$ *[1 mark]*

   c) $\frac{x}{5} = 4$
      $x = 4 \times 5 = 20$ *[1 mark]*

   d) $6 = \frac{42}{x}$
      $6x = 42$
      $x = 42 \div 6 = 7$ *[1 mark]*

2 a) $p - 11 = -7$
      $p = -7 + 11 = 4$ *[1 mark]*

   b) $2y - 5 = 9$
      $2y = 9 + 5 = 14$ *[1 mark]*
      $y = 14 \div 2 = 7$ *[1 mark]*
      [2 marks available in total — as above]

   c) $3z + 2 = z + 15$
      $3z - z = 15 - 2$
      $2z = 13$ *[1 mark]*
      $z = 13 \div 2 = 6.5$ *[1 mark]*
      [2 marks available in total — as above]

3 a) $3x + 5 = 14$
      $3x = 14 - 5 = 9$ *[1 mark]*
      $x = 9 \div 3 = 3$ *[1 mark]*
      [2 marks available in total — as above]

   b) $7x - 4 = 2x + 1$
      $7x - 2x = 1 + 4$
      $5x = 5$ *[1 mark]*
      $x = 5 \div 5 = 1$ *[1 mark]*
      [2 marks available in total — as above]

4 a) $40 - 3x = 17x$
      $40 = 17x + 3x$
      $40 = 20x$ *[1 mark]*
      $x = 40 \div 20 = 2$ *[1 mark]*
      [2 marks available in total — as above]

   b) $2y - 5 = 3y - 12$
      $-5 + 12 = 3y - 2y$ *[1 mark]*
      $y = 7$ *[1 mark]*
      [2 marks available in total — as above]

5 a) $3(a + 2) = 15$
      $(3 \times a) + (3 \times 2) = 15$
      $3a + 6 = 15$ *[1 mark]*
      $3a = 15 - 6$
      $3a = 9$ *[1 mark]*
      $a = 9 \div 3 = 3$ *[1 mark]*
      [3 marks available in total — as above]

   b) $2b - 6 = 2(3b + 1)$
      $2b - 6 = 6b + 2$ *[1 mark]*
      $-6 - 2 = 6b - 2b$
      $-8 = 4b$ *[1 mark]*
      $b = -8 \div 4 = -2$ *[1 mark]*
      [3 marks available in total — as above]

6 a) $5(2c - 1) = 4(3c - 2)$
      $10c - 5 = 12c - 8$ *[1 mark]*
      $-5 + 8 = 12c - 10c$
      $3 = 2c$ *[1 mark]*
      $c = 3 \div 2 = 1.5$ *[1 mark]*
      [3 marks available in total — as above]

   b) $(2p + 14) = \frac{2}{3}(1 - p)$
      $3(2p + 14) = 2(1 - p)$
      $6p + 42 = 2 - 2p$ *[1 mark]*
      $8p = -40$ *[1 mark]*
      $p = -5$ *[1 mark]*
      [3 marks available in total — as above]

Pages 33-34: Writing Equations

1 $8x - 5 = 3x$ *[1 mark]*
   $5x = 5$ *[1 mark]*
   $x = 1$ *[1 mark]*
   [3 marks available in total — as above]

2 $\frac{x}{2} + 20 = 3x$ *[1 mark]*
   $x + 40 = 6x$
   $5x = 40$
   $x = 8$
   So Alexa's original number was 8. *[1 mark]*
   [2 marks available in total — as above]

3 a) $f - 12$ *[1 mark]*

   b) $f + 7$ *[1 mark]*

   c) $4f - 3$ *[1 mark]*

4 $3X = Y$ *[1 mark]*
   $X + 9 = Y + 3$ *[1 mark]*
   $X + 9 = 3X + 3$
   $6 = 2X$
   $3 = X$
   So X = 3 g *[1 mark]* and Y = 3 × 3 = 9 g *[1 mark]*
   [4 marks available in total — as above]

5 $(x + 15°) + (x + 60°) + 3x = 180°$ *[1 mark]*
   $5x + 75° = 180°$ *[1 mark]*
   $5x = 105°$
   $x = 21°$ *[1 mark]*
   Therefore largest angle = $x + 60° = 81°$ *[1 mark]*
   [4 marks available in total — as above]

Pages 35-36: Formulas

1 $Q = 7x - 3y$
   $Q = (7 \times 8) - (3 \times 7)$
   $Q = 56 - 21 = 35$
   [2 marks available — 1 mark for correct substitution of x and y, 1 mark for correct final answer]

2 $S = 4m^2 + 2.5n$
   $S = (4 \times 6.5 \times 6.5) + (2.5 \times 4)$
   $S = 169 + 10$
   $S = 179$
   [2 marks available — 1 mark for correct substitution of m and n, 1 mark for correct final answer]

3 $F = \dfrac{9C}{5} + 32$
   $F = (9 \times 35 \div 5) + 32$
   $F = 95\ °F$
   [2 marks available — 1 mark for correct substitution of C, 1 mark for correct final answer]

4 a) Cost $= (£7 \times 13) + £25$
         $= £91 + £25 = £116$
       [2 marks available — 1 mark for correct substitution into formula, 1 mark for correct final answer]

   b) Cost $= (£2 \times 3) + (£5 \times 5)$
         $= £6 + £25 = £31$
       [2 marks available — 1 mark for correct substitution into formula, 1 mark for correct final answer]

5 Cost $= £300 + (\text{cost per day} \times \text{number of days})$
        $= £300 + (£50 \times 3)$
        $= £300 + £150 = £450$
   [2 marks available — 1 mark for correct substitution into formula, 1 mark for correct final answer]

6 Number of miles $= (\text{number of kilometres} \div 8) \times 5$
                    $= (110 \div 8) \times 5$
                    $= 68.75$
   [2 marks available — 1 mark for correct substitution into formula, 1 mark for correct final answer]

7 $m = 3p + 4$
   $3p = m - 4$ *[1 mark]*
   $p = \dfrac{m - 4}{3}$ *[1 mark]*
   [2 marks available in total — as above]

8 a) $u = v - at$ *[1 mark]*
   b) $v - u = at$ *[1 mark]*
       $t = \dfrac{v - u}{a}$ *[1 mark]*
       [2 marks available in total — as above]

Pages 37-38: Number Patterns and Sequences

1 a) 36, 44 *[1 mark]*
   b) 25, 33 *[1 mark]*

2 a) 8, 13, 18, 23, 28, 33, 38
       Rule: add 5 each time.
       [2 marks available — 1 mark for all correct terms, 1 mark for the correct rule]

   b) 3, 6, 12, 24, 48, 96
       Rule: double the previous number each time.
       [2 marks available — 1 mark for all correct terms, 1 mark for the correct rule]

3 a) There are 16 circles in pattern 8. *[1 mark]*
       There are 2 circles in pattern 1, 4 circles in pattern 2 and 6 circles in pattern 3 — so there are always 2n circles in the nth pattern of the sequence.

   b) E.g. number of straight lines in a pattern = number of circles – 1
       [1 mark]
       So, number of straight lines in the pattern with 22 circles
       $= (22 \times 2) - 1 = 44 - 1 = 43$ *[1 mark]*
       [2 marks available in total — as above]

4 a)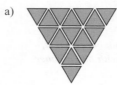
       [1 mark]

   b) n^2 *[1 mark]*

5 a) $1^2 + 4 = 5$ *[1 mark]*
   b) $8^2 + 4 = 68$ *[1 mark]*

6 2   9   16   23
     +7   +7   +7

   The common difference is 7, so $7n$ is in the formula.
   $$n = 1 \quad 2 \quad 3 \quad 4$$
   $$7n = 7 \quad 14 \quad 21 \quad 28$$
   $$|{-5} \quad |{-5} \quad |{-5} \quad |{-5}$$
   nth term $= 2 \quad 9 \quad 16 \quad 23$
   You have to subtract 5 to get to the term.
   So the expression for the nth term is $7n - 5$.
   [2 marks available — 2 marks for the correct expression, otherwise 1 mark for 7n]

7 3   7   11   15   19
     +4   +4   +4   +4

   The common difference is 4, so $4n$ is in the formula.
   $$4n = 4 \quad 8 \quad 12 \quad 16 \quad 20$$
   $$|{-1} \quad |{-1} \quad |{-1} \quad |{-1} \quad |{-1}$$
   nth term $= 3 \quad 7 \quad 11 \quad 15 \quad 19$

   You have to subtract 1 to get to the term.
   So the expression for the nth term is $4n - 1$.
   [2 marks available — 2 marks for the correct expression, otherwise 1 mark for 4n]

Page 39: Trial and Improvement

1
x	$x^3 + 4x$	
2	$2^3 + (4 \times 2) = 8 + 8 = 16$	Too small
3	$3^3 + (4 \times 3) = 27 + 12 = 39$	Too big
2.5	$2.5^3 + (4 \times 2.5) = 25.625$	Too big
2.3	$2.3^3 + (4 \times 2.3) = 21.367$	Too small
2.4	$2.4^3 + (4 \times 2.4) = 23.424$	Too small
2.45	$2.45^3 + (4 \times 2.45) = 24.506...$	Too big

So the solution is between $x = 2.4$ and $x = 2.45$,
so to 1 d.p. the solution is $x = 2.4$
[4 marks available — 1 mark for any trial between 2 and 3, 1 mark for any trial between 2.4 and 2.5 inclusive, 1 mark for a different trial between 2.43 and 2.45 inclusive, 1 mark for the correct final answer]

2
x	$x^3 - 2x$	
1	$1^3 - (2 \times 1) = 1 - 2 = -1$	Too small
2	$2^3 - (2 \times 2) = 8 - 4 = 4$	Too big
1.5	$1.5^3 - (2 \times 1.5) = 0.375$	Too big
1.3	$1.3^3 - (2 \times 1.3) = -0.403$	Too small
1.4	$1.4^3 - (2 \times 1.4) = -0.056$	Too small
1.45	$1.45^3 - (2 \times 1.45) = 0.148...$	Too big

The solution is between $x = 1.4$ and $x = 1.45$,
so to 1 d.p. the solution is $x = 1.4$
[4 marks available — 1 mark for any trial between 1 and 2, 1 mark for any trial between 1.4 and 1.5 inclusive, 1 mark for a different trial between 1.42 and 1.45 inclusive, 1 mark for the correct final answer]

Answers

Page 40: Inequalities

1 −3, −2, −1, 0, 1
   [2 marks available — 2 marks for all 5 numbers correct,
   otherwise 1 mark for the correct answer with one number
   missing or one number incorrect]

2 $2a - 7 \leq 11$
   $2a \leq 11 + 7$
   $2a \leq 18$ *[1 mark]*
   $a \leq 18 \div 2$
   $a \leq 9$ *[1 mark]*
   [2 marks available in total — as above]

3 a) $2p > 4$
       $p > 4 \div 2$
       $p > 2$ *[1 mark]*
   b) $4q - 5 < 23$
       $4q < 23 + 5$
       $4q < 28$ *[1 mark]*
       $q < 28 \div 4$
       $q < 7$ *[1 mark]*
       [2 marks available in total — as above]
   c) $4r - 2 \geq 2r + 5$
       $4r - 2r \geq 5 + 2$
       $2r \geq 7$ *[1 mark]*
       $r \geq 7 \div 2$
       $r \geq 3.5$ *[1 mark]*
       [2 marks available in total — as above]

4 a) $3x + 20 < 5x + 4$ *[1 mark]*
   b) $3x + 20 < 5x + 4$
       $20 - 4 < 5x - 3x$ *[1 mark]*
       $16 < 2x$ *[1 mark]*
       $x > 8$, so there are more than 8 lollipops in each packet. *[1 mark]*
       [3 marks available in total — as above]

Section Three — Graphs

Pages 41-42: Coordinates and Midpoints

1 a) (2, 1) *[1 mark]*
   b) (3, −2) *[1 mark]*
   c)
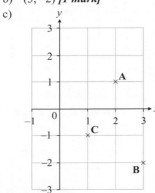
       [1 mark]

2 a) (1, 3) *[1 mark]*
   b) (1, 0) *[2 marks available — 2 marks for the correct answer,*
       otherwise 1 mark for correctly drawing point S on graph]
   c) (0, 4) *[2 marks available — 2 marks for the correct answer,*
       otherwise 1 mark for correctly drawing point T on graph]

3 C: (−3, −1) *[1 mark]*
   D: (−5, 3) *[1 mark]*
   [2 marks available in total — as above]

4 a)
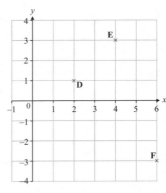
       [1 mark]
   b) $\left(\dfrac{2+4}{2}, \dfrac{1+3}{2}\right) = (3, 2)$
       [2 marks available — 1 mark for correct method and
       1 mark for correct final answer]
   c) $\left(\dfrac{2+6}{2}, \dfrac{1+(-3)}{2}\right) = (4, -1)$
       [2 marks available — 1 mark for correct method and 1 mark
       for correct final answer]

Pages 43-44: Straight-Line Graphs

1 a)
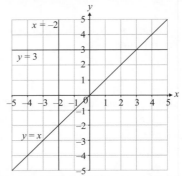
       [3 marks available — 1 mark for each correct line]
   b) (3, 3) *[1 mark]*

2 a)

x	−2	−1	0	1	2
y	−8	−5	−2	1	**4**

   [2 marks available — 2 marks for all values correct,
   otherwise 1 mark for 2 correct values]

   b)
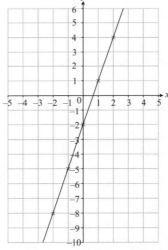

   [2 marks available — 2 marks for all points plotted correctly
   and a straight line drawn from (−2, −8) to (2, 4), otherwise
   1 mark for a correct straight line that passes through at least
   3 correct points, or a straight line with the correct gradient, or
   a straight line with a positive gradient passing through (0, −2)]

c)

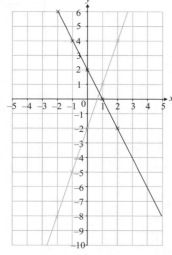

[3 marks available — 3 marks for a correct line drawn from (–2, 6) to (2, –2), otherwise 2 marks for a line that passes through (0, 2) and has a gradient of –2, or 1 mark for a line passing through (0, 2), or a line with a gradient of –2]

3 a)

x	–2	–1	0	1	2
y	14	11	8	5	**2**

[2 marks available — 2 marks for all values correct, otherwise 1 mark for 2 correct values]

b)

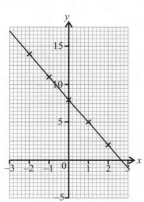

[2 marks available — 2 marks for all points plotted correctly and a straight line drawn from (–2, 14) to (2, 2), otherwise 1 mark for a correct straight line that passes through at least 3 correct points, or a straight line with the correct gradient, or a straight line with a negative gradient passing through (0, 8)]

4 a) $y = 4x – 1$ *[1 mark]*

b) E.g. No, they are not parallel because they do not have the same gradient. *[1 mark]*

Pages 45-46: Travel Graphs

1 a) $\frac{15-0}{1-0} = \frac{15}{1} = 15$ km/h

[2 marks available — 1 mark for a correct method, 1 mark for correct final answer]

b) The speed at which Selby was travelling. *[1 mark]*

c) 3 hours *[1 mark]*

As he was at point A at 0 hours, all you have to do is read off the x-value at point C to see how long Selby's journey was.

d) 2.5 hours *[1 mark]*

e)

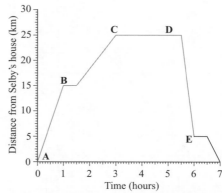

[2 marks available — 1 mark for a flat line from point E for 30 minutes, and 1 mark for a straight line from the end of the flat line to (7, 0)]

f) $7 – 0.5 – 2.5 – 0.5 = 3.5$ hours *[1 mark]*

Selby isn't cycling whenever the graph shows a horizontal line. So, subtract these times from the total amount of time he is out.

2 a) 3 pm *[1 mark]*

b) 120 – 100 *[1 mark]* = 20 miles *[1 mark]*

[2 marks available in total — as above]

3 a) Distance at 10:00 = 24 km

Distance at 11:00 = 48 km

So distance travelled = 48 – 24 = 24 km

[2 marks available — 1 mark for correctly reading both values off the graph, 1 mark for the correct final answer]

b) Average speed = distance ÷ time = 120 km ÷ 6 hours *[1 mark]*

= 20 km/h *[1 mark]*

[2 marks available in total — as above]

Pages 47-48: Real-Life Graphs

1 a) 36 litres (allow 35 – 37 litres) *[1 mark]*

b) 4.5 gallons (allow 4.3 – 4.5 gallons) *[1 mark]*

c) 40 litres = 8.8 gallons (allow 8.6 – 9.0 gallons)

40 × 2 = 80, so 8.8 gallons × 2 = 17.6 gallons

(allow 17.2 – 18.0 gallons)

[3 marks available — 1 mark for correct conversion factor, 1 mark for correct application of the conversion factor and 1 mark for answer within the range 17.2 – 18.0]

2 a) °F

[2 marks available — 2 marks for all 3 points plotted correctly and a straight line drawn through the points, otherwise 1 mark for at least 1 point plotted correctly and a straight line drawn through points]

b) 78 °F *[1 mark for an answer between 78 °F and 80 °F]*

c) 36 °C *[1 mark for an answer between 34 °C and 36 °C]*

3 a) Euros = 180 × 1.25 *[1 mark]*

= €225 *[1 mark]*

[2 marks available in total — as above]

b) Pounds = 48 ÷ 1.25 *[1 mark]*

= £38.40 *[1 mark]*

[2 marks available in total — as above]

c)

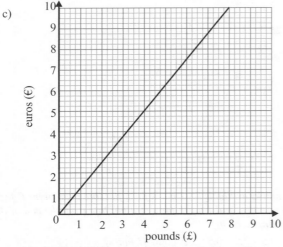

4   E.g. convert stone to lb: 1 stone = 14 lb *[1 mark]*
    so, 5.5 stone = 14 × 5.5 = 77 lb *[1 mark]*
    Convert lb to kg: 11 lb = 5 kg *[1 mark]*
    so, 77 lb = 5 × 7 = 35 kg (allow 34 – 36 kg) *[1 mark]*
    [4 marks available in total — as above]

Page 49: Quadratic Graphs

1   a)

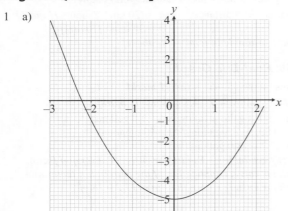

[2 marks available — 1 mark if all points are plotted correctly, 1 mark for a smooth curve joining the correctly plotted points]

b)   –2.2 (allow –2.3 to –2.1) *[1 mark]*

2   a)

x	–4	–3	–2	–1	0	1	2
y	8	3	0	–1	0	3	8

[1 mark]

b)

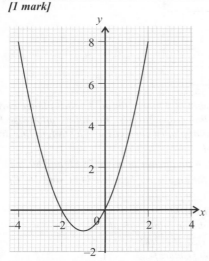

[2 marks available — 1 mark if all points are plotted correctly, 1 mark for a smooth curve joining the correctly plotted points]

c)   1.6 metres (allow 1.5 – 1.8 metres)
    [2 marks available — 1 mark for indicating 6 on the y-axis, 1 mark for the correct final answer]
    If the width of the pool is x and the length is (x + 2), then the area is x(x + 2), and you can use the graph to find when x(x + 2) = 6.

Page 50: Cubic Graphs

1   a)

x	–3	–2	–1	0	1	2	3
y	–19	0	7	8	9	16	35

[3 marks available — 1 mark for each correct y-value]

b)

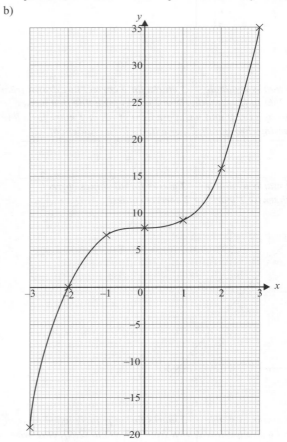

[2 marks available — 1 mark for plotting all points correctly, 1 mark for a smooth curve passing through all points]

Section Four — Shapes and Area

Pages 51-52: Symmetry and Tessellations

1   a)

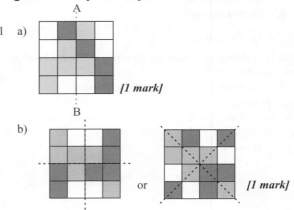

[1 mark]

b)

or   *[1 mark]*

c)
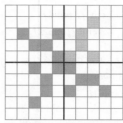

[3 marks available in total — 1 mark for the correct pattern in each section]

2 a) A and B
[2 marks available — 1 mark for each correct letter]

b) E *[1 mark]*

c) *[1 mark]*

3 a)
[2 marks available — 1 mark for each correct line of symmetry]

b) 2 *[1 mark]*

Page 53: Properties of 2D Shapes

1 a) Isosceles triangle *[1 mark]*
You need to say "isosceles triangle" to get the mark, not just "triangle".

b) C *[1 mark]*

2 E.g.
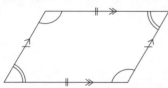

[2 marks available — 1 mark for 2 pairs of equal sides, 1 mark for 2 pairs of equal angles]
Read the information carefully — there's only one type of shape this could be.

3 E.g.
 [1 mark]

There isn't just one right answer here — as long as your shape has four sides, with two of them parallel, you'll get the mark.

4 a) No lines of symmetry *[1 mark]*

b) Order 2 *[1 mark]*

Page 54: Congruence and Similarity

1
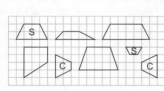

a) *[1 mark for shapes correctly labelled 'C' — as above]*
b) *[1 mark for shapes correctly labelled 'S' — as above]*

2 a) Triangle *AEX* *[1 mark]*

b) Triangle *AYX* *[1 mark]*

3 A and F *[1 mark]*
C and D *[1 mark]*
[2 marks available in total — as above]

Page 55: 3D Shapes

1 A = Sphere *[1 mark]*
B = Cone *[1 mark]*
[2 marks available in total — as above]

2 a) 6 *[1 mark]*

b) 12 *[1 mark]*

c) 8 *[1 mark]*

3 a) Pyramid or square-based pyramid *[1 mark]*

b) 6 *[1 mark]*

c) B *[1 mark]*

d) D *[1 mark]*

Page 56: Projections

1
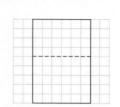

[3 marks available — 1 mark for a width of 6 squares, 1 mark for a height of 9 squares, 1 mark for a correct dotted or solid line marking the edge of the roof]

2
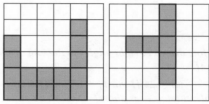

Front elevation   Plan view
[4 marks available in total — 2 marks for a correct front elevation diagram, otherwise 1 mark for a correct shape with one error in dimensions, and 2 marks for a correct plan view diagram in any orientation, otherwise 1 mark for a T-shaped diagram with the wrong dimensions]

3
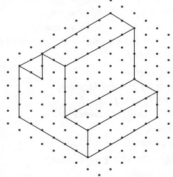

[2 marks available in total — 2 marks for a correct diagram, otherwise 1 mark for the correct cross-section but wrong length]

Pages 57-58: Perimeters and Areas

1 Answers between 16 and 20 cm^2 accepted
[2 marks available — 1 mark for a number within the range 16-20, 1 mark for the correct units]

2 a) 18 cm *[1 mark]*

b) 14 cm^2 *[1 mark]*

3 a) $6.4 \times 10 = 64$ cm^2
[2 marks available — 1 mark for correct calculation, 1 mark for correct answer]

b) $\sqrt{64} = 8$ cm
[2 marks available — 1 mark for correct calculation, 1 mark for correct answer]

Answers

4   Area of field = ½ × (105 + 80) × 60 = 5550 m² *[1 mark]*
Price of weedkiller per m² = 0.27 ÷ 10 = £0.027 *[1 mark]*
Cost = area × price per square metre = 5550 × 0.027 *[1 mark]*
= £149.85 *[1 mark]*
[4 marks available in total — as above]

5 a) Area of patio = 5 × 5 = 25 m² *[1 mark]*
      Area of lawn and patio = 27 × 10 = 270 m² *[1 mark]*
      Area of lawn = 270 – 25 = 245 m² *[1 mark]*
      245 ÷ 10 = 24.5, so 25 boxes needed. *[1 mark]*
      Cost = no. of boxes × price per box = 25 × 7 *[1 mark]*
      = £175.00 *[1 mark]*
      [6 marks available in total — as above]

   b) Perimeter of lawn = 10 + 22 + 5 + 5 + 5 + 27 = 74 m *[1 mark]*
      No. of strips = perimeter ÷ length of strip = 74 ÷ 2 *[1 mark]*
      = 37 strips *[1 mark]*
      [3 marks available in total — as above]

Pages 59-60: Circles

1 a) Diameter *[1 mark]*

   b) Radius *[1 mark]*

   c) Chord *[1 mark]*

   d)
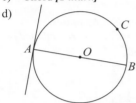
      [1 mark for line drawn at right angles to the end of the
      diameter at A]

2   Circumference = 2 × π × 0.25 *[1 mark]* = 1.57 m *[1 mark]*
     [2 marks available in total — as above]

3 a) 19.5 × 13 *[1 mark]* = 253.5 cm² *[1 mark]*
      [2 marks available in total — as above]

   b) Radius of biscuit = 13 ÷ 4 = 3.25 cm *[1 mark]*
      Area of biscuit = πr^2 = π × 3.25² *[1 mark]*
      = 33.2 cm² (to 1 d.p.) *[1 mark]*
      [3 marks available in total — as above]

4   Area of whole circle = π × 9.2² = 265.90... mm² *[1 mark]*
   Area of semicircle = 265.90... ÷ 2 = 132.95... mm² *[1 mark]*
                         = 133.0 mm² (1 d.p.) *[1 mark]*
   [3 marks available in total — as above]

5   Area of square = 8 × 8 = 64 m² *[1 mark]*
   Area of circle = π × 4² *[1 mark]* = 50.26... m² *[1 mark]*
   Area of grass = 64 – 50.26... = 13.73... m² *[1 mark]*
   No. of packets = 13.73... ÷ 0.5 = 27.469... *[1 mark]*
   So he will need 28 packets. *[1 mark]*
   [6 marks available in total — as above]

6   Area of cookie = π × 5² *[1 mark]* = 78.53... cm² *[1 mark]*
   78.53... ÷ 3 *[1 mark]* = 26.17... *[1 mark]*
   So the maximum number of buttons is 26. *[1 mark]*
   [5 marks available in total — as above]

Pages 61-62: Volume

1   Area of cross-section is 7 squares and the length is 3 cubes,
   so volume = 7 × 3 = 21 cm³
   [2 marks available — 1 mark for correct method,
   1 mark for correct answer]

2   Volume = 6 × 10 × 14 = 840 cm³
   [2 marks available — 1 mark for correct calculation,
   1 mark for correct answer]

3   Area of cross-section = π × 1² = 3.141... m² *[1 mark]*
   Volume of paddling pool = height × area of cross-section
   = 0.4 × 3.141... *[1 mark]*
   = 1.26 m³ (to 2 d.p.) *[1 mark]*
   [3 marks available in total — as above]

4   Area of cross-section = $\frac{1}{2}$ × 6 × 4 = 12 cm² *[1 mark]*
   Volume of prism = 12 × 4 *[1 mark]* = 48 cm³ *[1 mark]*
   [3 marks available in total — as above]

5 a) Volume = 90 × 40 × 30 *[1 mark]* = 108 000 cm³ *[1 mark]*
      [2 marks available in total — as above]

   b) Number of fish = 108 000 ÷ 6000 = 18
      So the greatest number of fish the tank can hold is 18.
      [2 marks available — 1 mark for correct calculation,
      1 mark for correct answer]

6   40 ÷ 8 = 5, so exactly 5 boxes fit into the width of each case.
   16 ÷ 8 = 2, so exactly 2 boxes fit into the height of each case.
   50 ÷ 8 = 6.25, so you can only fit 6 boxes along the length of the
   case, with a small gap at the end.
   So each case can take a maximum of 5 × 2 × 6 = 60 boxes of fudge.
   [3 marks available — 1 mark for a correct method, 1 mark for at
   least one division correct, and 1 mark for the correct final answer]
   You need to think practically here — if you divided the volume of the
   case by the volume of one box, you'd get 62.5. But you can't put bits of
   boxes in to fill gaps. So you need to stop and think about what the best
   way of packing whole boxes into the case is.

Pages 63-64: Nets

1   E.g.
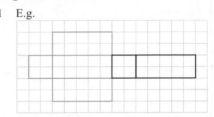
   [2 marks available — 1 mark for each correctly drawn side]

2   A *[1 mark]*

3 a) E.g.
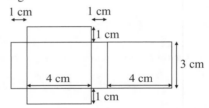
      [3 marks available in total — 3 marks for a correct and
      accurately drawn diagram, otherwise 1 mark for a net of any
      cuboid, or 2 marks for a net with five faces correct]
      There are several ways to make a cuboid net, so the faces in your
      net could be in different places relative to each other.

   b) Area of front = 4 × 1 = 4 cm²
      Area of side = 3 × 1 = 3 cm²
      Area of top = 4 × 3 = 12 cm²
      Total surface area = 2 × (4 + 3 + 12) = 38 cm²
      [3 marks available — 1 mark for finding the area of each face,
      1 mark for adding the areas, 1 mark for the correct final answer]

4
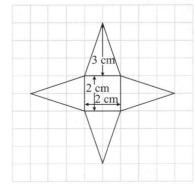
   [3 marks available in total — 3 marks for a correct and accurately
   drawn diagram, otherwise 1 mark for a square and 4 triangles with
   the wrong measurements, or 2 marks for a correctly-sized square
   and 4 isosceles triangles with the wrong measurements]

Answers

5   Surface area = $(2 \times 2\,\text{m} \times 1\,\text{m}) + (2 \times 2\,\text{m} \times 0.03\,\text{m}) +$
    $(2 \times 1\,\text{m} \times 0.03\,\text{m}) = 4.18\,\text{m}^2$
    Dan needs enough varnish to cover $4.18\,\text{m}^2 \times 2 = 8.36\,\text{m}^2$.
    $8.36\,\text{m}^2 \div 2.45\,\text{m}^2 = 3.4122...$ tins. So Dan should buy 4 tins.
    *[4 marks available — 1 mark for a correct method for finding the
    surface area, 1 mark for the correct surface area, 1 mark for a
    correct method for calculating the number of tins, and 1 mark for
    the correct final answer]*
    *Don't forget you need to round up here — not down. 3 tins wouldn't be
    enough, since you've worked out that Dan needs 3.4122... tins.*

6   Area of triangle = $\frac{1}{2} \times 6.0 \times 5.2 = 15.6\,\text{cm}^2$
    Area of whole octahedron = $8 \times 15.6 = 124.8\,\text{cm}^2$
    *[3 marks available — 1 mark for a correct method for finding the
    area of the triangle, 1 mark for the correct triangle area, 1 mark
    for the correct final answer]*

Section Five — Angles and Geometry

Pages 65-66: Measuring and Drawing Lines and Angles

1   a) 11 cm *[1 mark, allow ± 1 mm]*
    b) A————————————X————————————B *[1 mark]*
        Measure to check your cross is 5.5 cm from either end.

2   a)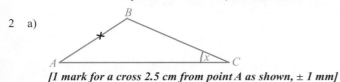
        [1 mark for a cross 2.5 cm from point A as shown, ± 1 mm]
    b) 9 cm *[1 mark, allow ± 1 mm]*
    c) 34° *[1 mark for any answer between 33° and 35°]*
    d) Acute angle *[1 mark]* *(writing 'acute' is OK too)*

3   Reflex angle *[1 mark]*

4   a)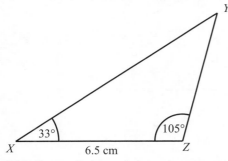
        [1 mark for either angle marked]
    b) 4.9 cm *[1 mark, allow ± 1 mm]*
    c) Obtuse angle *[1 mark]*
    d) 115° *[1 mark for any answer between 114° and 116°]*

5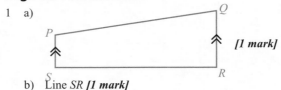
    (This diagram isn't actual size — but your measurements should
    match those given above.)
    *[3 marks available in total — 1 mark for a 6.5 cm line drawn
    (± 1 mm), 1 mark for correct angles drawn at the ends of this line
    (± 1°), 1 mark for a fully correct diagram]*
    *Measure to check the length of your lines and the size of your angles —
    make sure you've labelled your diagram too.*

Pages 67-68: Five Angle Rules

1   Angles on a straight line add up to 180°, so $x + 30° + 50° = 180°$.
    [1 mark]
    $x = 180° - 50° - 30° = 100°$. *[1 mark]*
    [2 marks available in total — as above]

2   $110° + 170° + 50° + 40° = 370°$. *[1 mark]*
    Angles round a point add up to 360°, not 370°, so these angles do
    not fit round a point as they are shown on the diagram. *[1 mark]*
    [2 marks available in total — as above]

3   a) $x + 60° + 74° = 180°$
        (angles in a triangle add up to 180°)
        So $x = 180° - 74° - 60° = 46°$
        *[2 marks available — 1 mark for a correct method,
        1 mark for the correct answer]*
    b) $x + y = 180°$ *(angles on a straight line add up to 180°)*
        $46° + y = 180°$, so $y = 180° - 46° = 134°$
        *[2 marks available — 1 mark for a correct method,
        1 mark for the correct answer]*

4   $360° - (2 \times 115°) = 130°$
    $130° \div 2 = 65°$
    *[2 marks available — 1 mark for a correct method,
    1 mark for the correct answer]*
    *Remember — angles in a quadrilateral add up to 360°,
    and parallelograms have 2 sets of equal angles.
    Using allied angles would also be a correct method here.*

5   $180° - 48° = 132° =$ Angles $ACB + BAC$ *[1 mark]*
    (angles in a triangle add up to 180°)
    Angle $ACB = 132° \div 2 = 66°$ *[1 mark]* *(ABC is isosceles)*
    Angle $BCD = 180° - 66° = 114°$ *[1 mark]*
    (angles on a straight line add up to 180°)
    [3 marks available in total — as above]

6   Angle $CBE = 180° - 115° = 65°$ *[1 mark]*
    Angle $BED = 180° - 103° = 77°$ *[1 mark]*
    because angles on a straight line add up to 180°. *[1 mark]*
    Angles in a quadrilateral add up to 360° *[1 mark]* so:
        $x + 90° + 77° + 65° = 360°$ *(CDE is a right angle)*
        $x + 232° = 360°$
            $x = 360° - 232° = 128°$ *[1 mark]*
    [5 marks available in total — as above]
    *Make sure you've answered this one in clear sentences,
    since you're marked on the quality of your written communication.*

7   Angles in a triangle add up to 180°. $180° - 96° = 84°$, *[1 mark]*
    so angle $VYX = 84° \div 2 = 42°$, because isosceles triangles have
    2 equal angles. *[1 mark]* Angles on a straight line add up to 180°,
    so angle $UYZ = 180° - 90° - 42°$ *[1 mark]* $= 48°$ *[1 mark]*
    [4 marks available in total — as above]

Page 69: Parallel Lines

1   a) *[1 mark]*
    b) Line SR *[1 mark]*

2   $a = 75°$ *[1 mark]* because vertically opposite angles are equal. *[1 mark]*
    [2 marks available in total — as above]

3   Angle $BDE = 117°$ *(corresponding angles)*
    Angle $CED = 30°$ *(vertically opposite angles)*
    Angle $CDE =$ Angle $CED = 30°$ *[1 mark]* *(isosceles triangle)*
    $x =$ Angle $BDE -$ Angle CDE *[1 mark]*
        $= 117° - 30° = 87°$ *[1 mark]*
    [3 marks available in total — as above]
    *There are other ways to find x. For instance, angle CBD =
    180° − 117° = 63° (angles on a straight line), angle BCD = CDE
    (alternate angles) = 30° (see above), so x = 180° − 63° − 30° = 87°
    (angles in a triangle).*

4 $a = 34°$ *[1 mark]* (corresponding angles)
   $b = 34°$ *[1 mark]* (alternate angles)
   $c = 62°$ *[1 mark]* (vertically opposite angles)
   $d = 180° - 62° = 118°$ *[1 mark]* (allied angles)
   [4 marks available in total — as above]

Page 70: Polygons and Angles

1 Number of sides = 8 *[1 mark]*
   Sum of interior angles = $(n - 2) \times 180°$ *[1 mark]*
   $= 6 \times 180° = 1080°$ *[1 mark]*
   Five of the angles are 117°, so the remaining 3 angles add up to:
   $1080° - (5 \times 117°)$ *[1 mark]*
   $= 495°$ *[1 mark]*
   The remaining 3 angles are all equal, so each angle is:
   $495° \div 3 = 165°$ *[1 mark]*
   [6 marks available in total — as above]
   You can use algebra to answer this question if you want to —
   just call the size of one of the remaining angles 'x'.

2 Exterior angle of a pentagon = $360° \div 5 = 72°$
   Interior angle of a pentagon = $180° - 72° = 108°$
   Angle in an equilateral triangle = $180° \div 3 = 60°$
   $p = 360° - (108° + 60°)$ *(angles round a point add up to 360°)*
   $= 360° - 168° = 192°$
   [4 marks available — 1 mark for calculating the interior angle
   of the pentagon, 1 mark for calculating the angle of the triangle,
   1 mark for using the 'angles around a point rule', 1 mark for the
   correct final answer]

3 Any quadrilateral can be split into two triangles by drawing a line
   between one pair of diagonally opposite corners. *[1 mark]*
   Angles in a triangle always add up to 180°. *[1 mark]*
   Therefore angles in a quadrilateral add up to $180° + 180° = 360°$.
   [1 mark]
   [3 marks available in total — as above]

Pages 71-73: Transformations

1
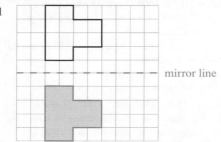
[1 mark]

2
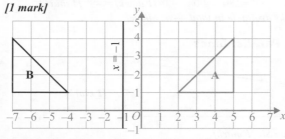
[2 marks available — 2 marks for correct reflection,
otherwise 1 mark for triangle reflected but in wrong position]

3 a)
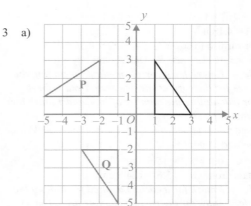
   [3 marks available — 3 marks for the correct rotation,
   otherwise 2 marks for a correct rotation but from the
   wrong centre, or 1 mark for 2 points correctly rotated]

   b) Rotation *[1 mark]* 90° anticlockwise *[1 mark]*
       about the origin *[1 mark]*
       [3 marks available in total — as above]

4 a) Translation *[1 mark]* 1 unit to the right and 7 units down.
       [1 mark].
       [2 marks available in total — as above]

   b)
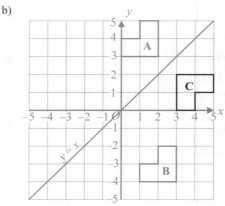
       [2 marks available — 2 marks for the correct reflection, otherwise
       1 mark for the correctly reflected shape in the wrong position]

   c) Rotation *[1 mark]* of 180° *[1 mark]* about the point (3, –1)
       [1 mark]
       [3 marks available in total — as above]

5 a)
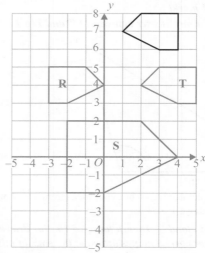
   [1 mark]

   b) Reflection *[1 mark]* in the line $x = 1$ *[1 mark]*.
       [2 marks available in total — as above]

   c) Enlargement *[1 mark]* of scale factor 2 *[1 mark]*,
       centre (–4, 8) *[1 mark]*.
       [3 marks available in total — as above]

6

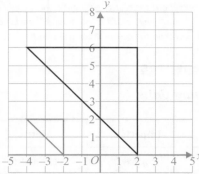

[3 marks available — 3 marks for correct enlargement, otherwise 2 marks for a correct triangle but in the wrong position or for an enlargement from the correct centre but of the wrong scale factor, or 1 mark for 2 lines enlarged by the correct scale factor anywhere on the grid]

7 Reflection in the *y*-axis / in the line *x* = 0.

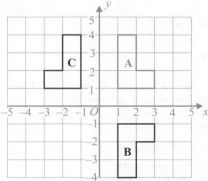

[4 marks available — 1 mark for correct position of B, 1 mark for correct position of C, 1 mark for reflection, 1 mark for mirror line]

Page 74: Triangle Construction

For these questions measure your construction to check it's accurately drawn.

1

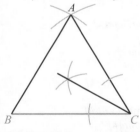

a) *[1 mark for correct arcs at point A with straight lines joining B and C to the point where they cross]*
b) *[2 marks available — 1 mark for compass arcs, 1 mark for bisector accurately drawn]*

2

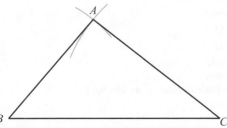

[3 marks available — 1 mark for BC within 1 mm of 5.6 cm, 1 mark for AB within 1 mm of 3.5 cm if correct construction arc is shown, 1 mark for AC within 1 mm of 4.3 cm if correct construction arc is shown]

Pages 75-76: Loci and Constructions

1

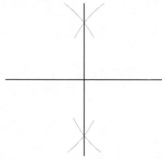

[2 marks available — 1 mark for two pairs of correct intersecting arcs, 1 mark for the correct line]

2

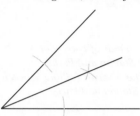

[2 marks available — 1 mark for two arcs, one on each line, that have been drawn from the same centre point, 1 mark for the correct bisector drawn through a correct pair of arcs]

3

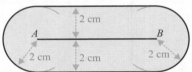

Scale: 1 cm represents 5 m
(diagram not actual size)
[2 marks available — 2 marks for arcs with a radius of 2 cm centred at A and B, lines 2 cm either side of AB and correct area shaded, otherwise 1 mark for arcs with a radius of 2 cm centred at A and B or for lines 2 cm either side of AB]
You'll still get the marks if you are within 1 mm of the correct measurements.

4

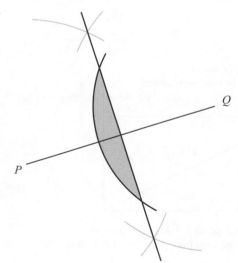

[3 marks available — 1 mark for a correct perpendicular bisector, mark for a correct arc 4.3 cm from Q that crosses the perpendicular bisector twice, 1 mark for shading the correct region]

Answers

5

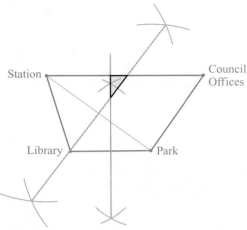

*[5 marks available — 1 mark for each pair of correct arcs
(centred at Library and Park and at Station and Park),
1 mark for each correct perpendicular bisector (of line between
Library and Park and line between Station and Park),
1 mark for correct shaded area]*

6

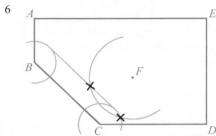

*[4 marks available — 1 mark for arcs with radius of 1 cm centred
at B and C, 1 mark for a line 1 cm from BC , 1 mark for an arc
with radius of 2 cm centred at F, 1 mark for correct crosses at the
intersections]*

Page 77: Pythagoras' Theorem

1   $2.5^2 + x^2 = 3.6^2$ *[1 mark]*
   $x^2 = 3.6^2 - 2.5^2$
   $x^2 = 6.71$
   $x = \sqrt{6.71}$ *[1 mark]*
   $x = 2.590...$
   $= 2.6$ m (to 1 d.p.) *[1 mark]*
   [3 marks available in total — as above]
   Giving your answer as '2.59 (to 2 d.p.)' will also get you the marks here.

2
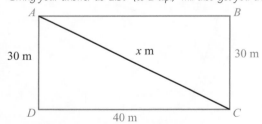

The garden is a rectangle, so the side AD is also 30 m.
The distance round the edge from A to C is 30 m + 40 m = 70 m.
[1 mark]
Let the distance across the diagonal from point A to point C be x m.
By Pythagoras' theorem $30^2 + 40^2 = x^2$ *[1 mark]*
$x = \sqrt{900 + 1600} = \sqrt{2500} = 50$ m *[1 mark]*
The price for laying the pipe across the diagonal is £8.35 per metre plus
the cost of digging the trench and replacing the grass:
   £202.50 + (50 × £8.35) = £620.00 *[1 mark]*
The price for laying the pipe around the edge is £8.35 per metre:
   70 × £8.35 = £584.50 *[1 mark]*
It is cheaper to lay the pipe round the edge — it will cost £620.00 to lay
the pipe across the diagonal and only £584.50 to lay it around the edge.
*[1 mark for concluding that it's cheaper to lay the pipe round the
edge, if the cost of each has been worked out above]*
[6 marks available in total — as above]

Alternatively, instead of working out the cost of each option, you could work
out the cost of the extra 20 m of pipe needed to go around the edge of the
field, and show that this is less than the cost of digging a trench.

Section Six — Measures

Pages 78-79: Converting Units

1   a)

	Imperial	Metric
Length of a skirt	inches	centimetres
Weight of a rabbit	pounds	kilograms
Volume of a milk jug	pints	litres

[3 marks available — 1 mark for each correct answer]
   b)   8.87 m *[1 mark]*
   c)   1300 g *[1 mark]*
2   a)   To the nearest gram *[1 mark]*
   b)   To the nearest tonne *[1 mark]*
3   2.5 litres × 1000 = 2500 ml
   2500 ÷ 250 = 10 cups
   *[3 marks available — 1 mark for converting litres to ml, 1 mark
   for dividing by 250, and 1 mark for final answer]*
   *A correct method here could also be to convert 250 ml into litres
   (0.25 litres) and then divide 2.5 by 0.25.*

4   a)   40 km into miles = $\frac{5 \times 40}{8}$ *[1 mark]*
                        = 25 miles *[1 mark]*
      [2 marks available in total — as above]
   b)   60 km/h into mph = $\frac{5 \times 60}{8}$ = 37.5 mph *[1 mark]*
      Since 37.5 mph is less than 40 mph, the camel would
      outrun a giraffe. *[1 mark]*
      [2 marks available in total — as above]
5   2500 g ÷ 1000 = 2.5 kg *[1 mark]*
   Convert kg into lb: 2.5 × 2.2 = 5.5 lb *[1 mark]*
   5.5 ÷ 1.5 = 3.6666... *[1 mark]*
   Maximum number of books = 3 *[1 mark]*
   [4 marks available in total — as above]
6   14 pints into litres: 14 ÷ 1.75 = 8 litres *[1 mark]*
   = 8000 ml *[1 mark]*
   (3 × 720 ml) + (5 × 520 ml) = 4760 ml *[1 mark]*
   8000 ml − 4760 ml = 3240 ml left *[1 mark]*
   3240 ÷ 540 = 6 times *[1 mark]*
   [5 marks available in total — as above]

Page 80: Reading Scales

1   a)   5 °C *[1 mark]*
   b)   78 mph *[1 mark]*
   c)   15 oz *[1 mark]*
2   a)   55 ml *[1 mark]*
   b)   55 − 15 *[1 mark]*
      = 40 ml *[1 mark]*
      [2 marks available in total — as above]
3   a)   40.6 m *[1 mark]*
   b)

[1 mark]

Page 81: Rounding and Estimating Measurements

1   Average height of a man ≈ 180 cm (allow 150 – 210 cm,
   or 5 ft – 6 ft 6 inches) *[1 mark]*
   height of penguin ≈ 180 ÷ 3 *[1 mark]*
   = 60 cm (accept 50 – 67 cm) *[1 mark]*
   [3 marks available in total — as above]

2 a) –1.6 °C *[1 mark]*
   b)

   [1 mark]
   c) 2.5 °C *[1 mark]*

3 Upper bound = 57.5 kg *[1 mark]*
  Lower bound = 56.5 kg *[1 mark]*
  [2 marks available in total — as above]

Pages 82-83: Reading Timetables

1 a) 11:15 am *[1 mark]*
  b) 10:30 am – 5 hrs = 5:30 am *[1 mark]*
2 a) 11:15 – 25 min *[1 mark]*
     = 10:50 *[1 mark]*
     [2 marks available in total — as above]
  b) 11:35 → 13:22 = 1 h 47 min *[1 mark]*
     = 107 minutes *[1 mark]*
     [2 marks available in total — as above]
3 a) 17 04 *[1 mark]*
  b) 6 minutes *[1 mark]*
  c) 16:40 → 18:15 *[1 mark]*
     = 1 h 35 mins *[1 mark]*
     [2 marks available in total — as above]
4 a) Britney *[1 mark]*
  b) 1 hour 30 minutes *[1 mark]*
  c) 18:30 to 18:45 *[1 mark]*
     and 20:00 to 20:30 *[1 mark]*
     [2 marks available in total — as above]
5 Paris is 8 hours ahead of San Francisco, so 07:15 – 8 hours = 23:15
  Time: 23:15
  Day: Wednesday
  [3 marks available — 3 marks for correct time and day, otherwise 2 marks for correct time difference and either correct time or day, otherwise 1 mark for correct time difference or time or day. Allow time given as 11:15 pm]

Page 84: Bearings and Maps

1 a) 035° (accept 034° – 036°) *[1 mark]*
  b)

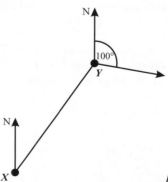

     [1 mark]
2 a) 4 × 200 000 = 800 000 cm = 8 km (allow 7.6 – 8.4 km) *[1 mark]*
  b) 7 km = 700 000 cm
     700 000 ÷ 200 000 = 3.5 cm *[1 mark]*

Page 85: Speed

1 speed = $\frac{distance}{time}$, so speed × time = distance *[1 mark]*
  = 56 × 1.25 = 70 km *[1 mark]*
  [2 marks available in total — as above]

2 a) Friday: speed = 5 ÷ 0.75 = 6.66... mph
     Saturday: speed = 26 ÷ 3.25 = 8 mph
     Sunday: speed = 33 ÷ 3.75 = 8.8 mph
     so, Beatrix rode fastest on Sunday
     [4 marks available — 1 mark for attempting to divide a distance by a time, 1 mark for getting one speed correct, 1 mark for getting the other two speeds correct, 1 mark for a correct final answer]

  b) Overall speed = $\frac{distance}{time}$ *[1 mark]*
     = $\frac{5 + 26 + 33}{0.75 + 3.25 + 3.75} = \frac{64}{7.75}$ *[1 mark]*
     = 8.3 mph (1 dp) *[1 mark]*
     [3 marks available in total — as above]

Section Seven — Statistics and Probability

Page 86: Collecting Data

1 E.g. No time frame is given. / The response boxes do not cover all possible outcomes. / The response boxes overlap.
  [2 marks available — 1 mark for each of the above, up to a maximum of 2]

2 a) E.g. No time frame is specified, so the response boxes are vague and could be interpreted differently by different people / the response boxes do not cover all possible answers.
     [1 mark]
  b) E.g. The results of his survey are likely to be biased as he is only asking boys who like football.
     [1 mark]

Page 87: Mean, Median, Mode and Range

1 a) In ascending order: 3, 10, 12, 12, 13, 18, 25, 33, 37, 41
     Median = (13 + 18) ÷ 2 = 15.5 minutes
     [2 marks available — 1 mark for ordering the numbers in ascending or descending order and 1 mark for correctly working out the median]
  b) Mean = (3 + 10 + 12 + 12 + 13 + 18 + 25 + 33 + 37 + 41) ÷ 10
     = 204 ÷ 10 *[1 mark]* = 20.4 minutes
     = 20 minutes (to the nearest minute) *[1 mark]*
     [2 marks available in total — as above]
  c) Range = 41 – 3 *[1 mark]* = 38 minutes *[1 mark]*
     [2 marks available in total — as above]

2 a) £18 000 *[1 mark]*
  b) £18 000 *[1 mark]*
  c) Mean for Company A
     = (18 000 + 18 000 + 18 000 + 25 200 + 38 500) ÷ 5
     = 117 700 ÷ 5 *[1 mark]* = £23 540 *[1 mark]*, so Company A has a lower mean annual salary than Company B. *[1 mark]*
     [3 marks available in total — as above]

3 1, 4, 7
  [2 marks available — 2 marks for all three numbers correct, otherwise 1 mark for 3 numbers that have a range of 6 and a mean of 4 but aren't all different, or 3 different numbers that add up to 12 or that have a range of 6]

146

Page 88: Tables

1 a) The Ivy *[1 mark]*

b) 2 *[1 mark]*

2 Cost in June = 2 × £300 + 3 × £290 = £1470
Cost in July = 2 × £330 + 3 × £275 = £1485
So it would be cheaper for the Whites to go for a week in June.
[4 marks available — 1 mark for multiplying by 2 for the adult price and by 3 for the child price, 1 mark for using the correct adult and child prices from the table, 1 mark for the correct total cost in June and the correct total cost in July, 1 mark for clearly stating that June is cheaper]

Page 89: Pictograms

1 a) 40 *[1 mark]*

b)

Strawberry Jam	🍓 🍓 🍓 🍓
Blackberry Jam	🍓 🍓 ◖
Raspberry Jam	🍓 🍓 🍓 ◖
🍓 Represents 10 jars

[1 mark]

c) Blackberry Jam *[1 mark]*

2 a) 30 *[1 mark]*

b) 40 − 20 = 20 *[1 mark]*

c)

| Thursday | ○ ○ ○ |
| Friday | ○ ○ ◿ |

[2 marks available — 1 mark for three full circles drawn for Thursday and 1 mark for two and a quarter circles drawn for Friday]

Page 90: Bar Charts

1 a) 25 *[1 mark]*

b) Tuesday *[1 mark]*

c)

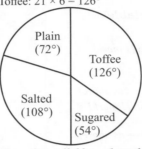

[2 marks available — 1 mark for a light shaded bar drawn to 45 and 1 mark for a dark shaded bar drawn to 30]

d) No. of cups of tea sold = 50 + 40 + 25 + 70 + 45 = 230
No. of cups of coffee sold = 30 + 55 + 60 + 50 + 30 = 225
So, there were more cups of tea sold in total.
[2 marks available — 1 mark for finding both totals, 1 mark for the correct answer]

2

[3 marks available — 1 mark for a suitable scale, 1 mark for a fully labelled bar chart, 1 mark for all bar heights correct]

Page 91: Pie Charts

1 a) $\frac{1}{4}$ *[1 mark]*

b) Badminton = 360 − 180 − 90 − 30 = 60°
Football = 180°, so 60 people = 180°
1 person = 180° ÷ 60 = 3°
So number of people who prefer badminton = 60° ÷ 3° = 20
[2 marks available — 1 mark for a correct method, 1 mark for the correct final answer]
There are other ways to work this out — e.g. you could also use the number of people who prefer football (60) to work out the total people surveyed and then use the angle of the badminton sector to work out what fraction of the total this is $\left(\frac{1}{6}\right)$.

2 a) Total number of people = 12 + 18 + 9 + 21 = 60
Multiplier = 360 ÷ 60 = 6
Plain: 12 × 6 = 72°
Salted: 18 × 6 = 108°
Sugared: 9 × 6 = 54°
Toffee: 21 × 6 = 126°

[3 marks available — 1 mark for a correct method, 1 mark for all angles drawn correctly ± 1°, 1 mark for correct labels]

b) E.g. Chris is not right because there is no information about the number of people in the ice-cream survey. *[1 mark]*

Page 92: Scatter Graphs

1 a) 62% *[1 mark]*

b) E.g.

[1 mark for line of best fit that lies between (12, 16) and (12, 28) and also between (80, 82) and (80, 96)]

c) 56%
[2 marks available — 1 mark for indicating 66 on the y-axis, 1 mark for the x-coordinate of the line of best fit when y = 66]

d) E.g. there is some strong support for this hypothesis *[1 mark]*

2 a)

[1 mark for both points plotted correctly]

Answers

b) Positive correlation *[1 mark]*

c) 72-74 kg
[2 marks available — 1 mark for line of best fit, 1 mark for an answer in the range 72-74 kg]

Page 93: Frequency Tables and Averages

1 a)

Drink	Tally	Frequency
Cola	IIII II	7
Orange juice	IIII	5
Lemonade	III	3
Other	IIII	5

[2 marks available — 2 marks if all the frequencies are correct, otherwise 1 mark if at least 2 frequencies are correct]

b) Cola *[1 mark]*

2 a) Total number of vehicles = 13 + 8 + 6 + 2 + 1 = 30, so the median is halfway between the 15th and 16th values *[1 mark]*, so the median = 1 *[1 mark]*
[2 marks available in total — as above]

b) $((13 \times 0) + (8 \times 1) + (6 \times 2) + (2 \times 3) + (1 \times 4)) \div 30$
$= (0 + 8 + 12 + 6 + 4) \div 30$
$= 30 \div 30 = 1$
[3 marks available — 1 mark for multiplying the vehicles per minute by the frequency and adding, 1 mark for dividing by 30, 1 mark for the correct final answer]

Page 94: Grouped Frequency Tables — Averages

1

Arm Span, x cm	Frequency	Mid-Interval Value	Frequency × Mid-Interval Value
$120 \leq x < 130$	13	$(120 + 130) \div 2$ $= 125$	$13 \times 125 =$ 1625
$130 \leq x < 140$	6	$(130 + 140) \div 2$ $= 135$	$6 \times 135 =$ 810
$140 \leq x < 150$	4	$(140 + 150) \div 2$ $= 145$	$4 \times 145 =$ 580
$150 \leq x < 160$	7	$(150 + 160) \div 2$ $= 155$	$7 \times 155 =$ 1085
Total	30		4100

So an estimate of the mean arm span is 4100 ÷ 30 = 136.6666...
= 137 cm (to the nearest cm.)
[4 marks available — 1 mark for the correct midpoints, 1 mark for using these to find frequency × mid-interval value, 1 mark for 4100 ÷ 30, 1 mark for the correct final answer]

2 a) Total number of children = 3 + 2 + 12 + 8 + 5 = 30, so the median value is halfway between the 15th and 16th values *[1 mark]*, so it is in the $9.5 \leq x < 10$ group *[1 mark]*
[2 marks available in total — as above]

b) $9.5 \leq x < 10$ *[1 mark]*

c)

Length of line, x cm	Frequency	Mid-Interval Value	Frequency × Mid-Interval Value
$8.5 \leq x < 9$	3	$(8.5 + 9) \div 2 =$ 8.75	$3 \times 8.75 =$ 26.25
$9 \leq x < 9.5$	2	$(9 + 9.5) \div 2 =$ 9.25	$2 \times 9.25 =$ 18.5
$9.5 \leq x < 10$	12	$(9.5 + 10) \div 2$ $= 9.75$	$12 \times 9.75 =$ 117
$10 \leq x < 10.5$	8	$(10 + 10.5) \div 2$ $= 10.25$	$8 \times 10.25 =$ 82
$10.5 \leq x < 11$	5	$(10.5 + 11) \div 2$ $= 10.75$	$5 \times 10.75 =$ 53.75
Total	30		297.5

So an estimate of the mean length is 297.5 ÷ 30 = 9.9166...
= 9.9 cm (to 1 d.p.)
[4 marks available — 1 mark for the correct midpoints, 1 mark for using these to find frequency × mid-interval value, 1 mark for dividing 297.5 by 30, 1 mark for the correct final answer]

Page 95: Frequency Polygons

1

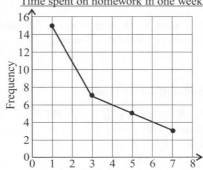

Time spent on homework in one week

Number of Hours of Homework

[2 marks available — 2 marks if all 4 points are plotted correctly and joined up, otherwise 1 mark if either the points are correct but not joined up, or if only 2 or 3 points are correct, or if the points have been plotted at the upper or lower class boundaries and joined up]

2 a) E.g. There was between 4 and 6 mm of rainfall more often in Holcombury than in Ramsbrooke.
[1 mark for any correct comparison]
There are quite a few other comparisons you could make here — for example, you could look at the total rainfall over the 45 days.

b) $(3 \times 1) + (5 \times 3) + (6 \times 5) + (13 \times 7) + (11 \times 9)$
$+ (6 \times 11) + (1 \times 13) = 3 + 15 + 30 + 91 + 99 + 66 + 13 = 317$
$317 \div 45 = 7.0444.... = 7.0$ mm (to 1 d.p.)
[3 marks available — 1 mark for multiplying the frequencies by the midpoints, 1 mark for dividing by 45, 1 mark for the correct final answer]

Page 96: More Charts and Graphs

1 a) E.g. the range for the sample from Liverchester is 8 – 1 = 7 and the range for the sample from Newpool is 5 – 1 = 4, so the range is greater for the sample from Liverchester.
[2 marks available — 1 mark for correctly finding at least one of the ranges, 1 mark for correctly indicating that the range for the sample from Liverchester is greater]

b) E.g. it may appear that the average income in Liverchester in 2010 was higher than the average income in Newpool in 2010, because the piggy bank for the average income in Liverchester in 2010 is much larger.
[2 marks available — 1 mark for any possible misunderstanding, 1 mark for a correct reason why]
You would get the marks here for any correct comment about the misleading sizes of the piggy banks. For example, you might choose to say that the diagram could make it appear that the average income in the two cities in 1990 was the same, because the piggy banks are the same size.

Pages 97-98: Probability Basics

1 a) unlikely *[1 mark]*
   b) evens *[1 mark]*
   c) impossible *[1 mark]*

2 a)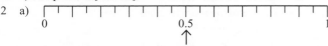

[1 mark]

   b)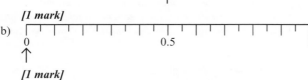

[1 mark]

   c) $\frac{2}{6} = \frac{1}{3}$
   [2 marks available — 1 mark for showing there are 2 chances out of 6, 1 mark for the correct simplified fraction]

3 a) Blue *[1 mark]*
   b) $\frac{3}{8}$ *[1 mark]*

4 a) Number of red counters = $10 - 4 = 6$ *[1 mark]*
      Probability of getting a red counter = $\frac{6}{10} = \frac{3}{5}$ *[1 mark]*
      [2 marks available in total — as above]
      If the question doesn't tell you how to give your answer, a correct decimal would gain full marks too.
   b) There are no green counters, so the probability of getting a green = 0 *[1 mark]*

5 Total number of people in the team = $6 + 9 + 4 + 1 = 20$ *[1 mark]*
   So the probability that person's favourite position is midfield
   = $\frac{9}{20}$ *[1 mark]*
   [2 marks available in total — as above]

6 $0.4 + x + 2x = 1$ *[1 mark]*
   $3x = 1 - 0.4 = 0.6$
   $x = 0.6 \div 3 = 0.2$ *[1 mark]*
   P(stripy sock) = $2x$, so P(stripy sock) = $2 \times 0.2 = 0.4$ *[1 mark]*
   [3 marks available in total — as above]

Page 99: More Probability

1 a)

Cards

		2	4	6	8	10
	1	3	5	7	9	11
	2	4	6	8	10	12
Dice	**3**	5	7	9	11	13
	4	6	8	10	12	14
	5	7	9	11	13	15
	6	8	10	12	14	16

[2 marks available — 2 marks if all entries are correct, otherwise 1 mark if at least 4 entries are correct]

b) 3 ways of scoring exactly 9
   Total number of possible outcomes = 30
   Probability of scoring exactly 9 = $\frac{3}{30}$ *[1 mark]*
   $= \frac{1}{10}$ *[1 mark]*
   [2 marks available in total — as above]

2 $0.23 + 0.28$ *[1 mark]*
   $= 0.51$ *[1 mark]*
   [2 marks available in total — as above]

Page 100: Expected Frequency

1 $200 \times 0.64 = 128$ times
   [2 marks available — 1 mark for a correct method, 1 mark for the correct final answer]

2 P(lands on 5) = 1 – P(lands on 1, 2, 3 or 4) *[1 mark]*
   P(lands on 5) = 1 – (0.3 + 0.15 + 0.2 + 0.25) = 0.1 *[1 mark]*
   Estimate of number of times spinner lands on 5 = 100×0.1 *[1 mark]*
   = 10 times *[1 mark]*
   [4 marks available in total — as above]

3 Number of easy games I should expect to win:
   $20 \times \frac{1}{2} = 10$, *[1 mark]* so I should expect to:
   gain $10 \times 3 = 30$ points and lose $(20 - 10) \times 2 = 10 \times 2 = 20$ points.
   So overall, I should expect to end up with $30 - 20 = 10$ points.
   [1 mark]
   Number of hard games I should expect to win:
   $20 \times \frac{1}{5} = 4$, *[1 mark]* so I should expect to:
   gain $4 \times 8 = 32$ points and lose $(20 - 4) \times 2 = 16 \times 2 = 32$ points.
   So overall, I should expect to end up with $32 - 32 = 0$ points. *[1 mark]*
   So I should expect to end up with 10 more points playing 20 easy games than playing 20 hard games. *[1 mark]*
   [5 marks available in total — as above]

Page 101: Relative Frequency

1 a) Relative frequency of no biscuit after 2000 bars = 0.0035
      $0.0035 \times 2000 = 7$ *[1 mark]*, so 7 bars had no biscuit, and $2000 - 7 = 1993$ bars had biscuit. *[1 mark]*
      [2 marks available in total — as above]
   b) The relative frequency of no biscuit after picking 4000 bars is the best estimate, this is because the more times you repeat an experiment the more accurate the relative frequency will be.
      [2 marks available — 1 mark for 4000 bars, 1 mark for an explanation that refers to a larger number of repeats giving a better estimate]

How to get answers for the Practice Papers

You can print out worked solutions to Practice Papers 1 & 2 by accessing your free Online Edition of this book (which also includes step-by-step video solutions).

There's more info about how to get your Online Edition at the front of this book.

MIFO41